R. NORTON
46 Leigh Furlong Rd
Street BA16-0LF
01458 443735

Sculptor in Wood

The collected woodcarvings of
Fred Cogelow

Sculptor in Wood

The collected woodcarvings of
Fred Cogelow

with
Comments by the Artist

Heart Prairie Press
Whitewater, Wisconsin

First Printing – July, 1991
Second Printing – November, 1991

Published by
Heart Prairie Press
P.O. Box 332
Whitewater, WI 53190

Printed in the United States of America.

Publisher's Cataloging in Publication Data
Cogelow, Fred, 1949-
    Sculptor in wood : the collected woodcarvings of Fred
Cogelow, with comments by the artist. --

    p. cm.
    ISBN 0-9622663-4-5

    1. Cogelow, Fred, 1949- 2. Sculpture. 3. Wood-carving.
I. Title.

NB237.C6   730.92
                                    QBI91-205

Dedication

To mother earth (woman, if she be, that I love most) — with a prayer that she forgive me for the offenses to her which the production of this publication has entailed.

Acknowledgements

I would like to acknowledge a few fine folks in my life who've made it possible for me to do such mean and nasty low-down things to innocent blocks of wood. Inspiration awards go to Otto Nygaard, my old Norskie wood-working neighbor; to Harold Strand, my late sawyer; to Adolph Highstrom, my north 40 bachelor Swede farmer-philosopher; and to my father who left me all those fascinating tools, the use of which I knew nothing about.

Special affection goes to my wife, mother and dogs for supporting me when I couldn't support myself. Deep gratitude goes to the McDonough, Haines and Carney tribes for their all-around support. Four of my early commissioners likewise warrant special mention, for their demands of me were critical to later successes. They are Bill Bernard, Dick Hazen, Pat Malone, and Lyle Munneke.

The deepest debt, perhaps, is to Bob Mischka, editor and publisher, for having conceived of this volume and pushed it to fruition.

Foreword
by Marion Nelson

It could be easy to think of Fred as a virtuoso carver because he is an absolute master of technique. Virtuosity, however, is a consequence rather than a goal in his work. What comes first is a human statement, and the technical proficiency results from wanting to make that statement as precise as possible. Being self-taught in woodcarving, Fred has developed his technique as the handmaid of what he has to say. This means that viewing a work by him is first and foremost an encounter with the subject. It is only after this encounter that one must ask what makes the presence of the subject so real.

The impact of the image in Fred's work is not the result of technique alone but of the process by which his work comes into being. Most of his subject matter since 1985 has been drawn from his immediate experience. The people who surround him are those who surround most of us, but we allow our impressions of them to slip into a memory bank where they remain dormant until aroused by a reminder. The majority of Fred's recent works are such reminders. In this sense they relate to the stories of Garrison Keillor that are also based on the common but half-forgotten experiences of a great many people. The impact is also similar but can be stronger in sculpture, which represents one moment, than in narrative, which spans a period of time.

Fred understands well the phenomenon of having a single image arouse composite memories because this also occurs in his own creative process. He tells us that the initial concept of "Gust — With Thoughts of Mabel" (p. 64) came from watching the shuffling German farmers in Paynesville, Minnesota, but that the subject did not take concrete form until he saw a photograph of a Missouri farmer in *National Geographic*. It resurrected in a suitable framework the dormant recollections from Paynesville. This is only one of several instances mentioned by Fred in which a specific pictorial image has pulled together broader concepts arrived at through experience. Fred then transfers this image to the public where it continues to do its work.

Another aspect of Fred's creative process that gives impact to the products of his hands is the early point at which the image is linked to a specific block of wood. Fred stockpiles material much as he does subject matter. He obtains any block in which he sees the potential of an image. Subject matter and material come together naturally and are made one through the work of the chisel. The fact that Fred learned to give his concepts form in wood without academic training in design or in working with other materials adds to the total unity of his works. No familiar technical devices or stylistic manners detract from his personal statement.

Even if technique is the means rather than the message in much of Fred's work, it is important. Fred has for the past eight years been walking the tight-rope between technical virtuosity and genuine artistic expression. His technique developed rapidly from the time he created the little figure "Albert the Alligator" (8) to his producing "Hunts the Crying Bear" (42) ten years later, which he considers as demanding "as anything you'll find being carved these days." The subject matter from this period, largely grotesques and Indians, now seems cliché, but Fred's youthful enthusiasm for it brought his technical achievement to towering heights. "Hunts the Crying Bear" is a powerfully romantic presentation of the Indian, but it is also, as Fred admits, a *tour de force* of the carver's art. It appealed and sold, a new experience for Fred. He could at this point easily have begun to ride on his technical achievements, but he chose instead to change direction. "It is all well and good . . . to throw in all sorts of trappings just to make life difficult for yourself. . . But that is not the same as capturing the spirit of an individual" (44). Capturing this spirit constitutes the essence of Fred's later work.

It is as a realist in wood that Fred is gaining a reputation. He is known as the artist who does not miss a detail or shun carving even free-hanging shoelaces. This reputation is deserved because he is phenomenal both in the observation and execution of detail. More significant in his figures than the details themselves, however, is the fact that they all find a natural place on a remarkably accurate treatment of the human anatomy. Fred's work represents a great variety of body positions, but all are convincing even when viewed from several angles. "Gust" (64) was created from a photograph which shows the figure from behind, and either the back or the front works equally well as the major side for viewing. "The Story's About Joe's Wife" (62), with its relaxed figure perched precariously on a bar stool, is the ultimate to date in Fred's mastery of presenting the human body. The unusual thing about that mastery is that it has been achieved through direct observation of people in action rather than through academic study of the figure and classic traditions in its presentation. This eliminates stereotype treatments and allows the individual characteristics of each body to become an expressive part of the work and give a sense of real presence to the subject. Both "Gust" and "Ed" (54) are striking examples.

But to stop with calling Fred a realist does not do him justice. A fascination for abstract design is reflected in much of his work and rates with the interpretation of character in accounting for its artistic significance. It was his abstract and semi-abstract pieces from 1974 (10-11) that first aroused my interest in Fred. They can be compared to work by Constantin Brancusi from the beginning of modernism around 1914; but while the sophisticated Brancusi was drawing inspiration from primitive sources, Fred was still a primitive who was creating works of remarkable sophistication. His "Untitled" (10) and "Stoic Ambiguity" (11), the latter of which was shown under a different title in Vesterheim's exhibition *Norwegian-American Wood Carving of the Upper Midwest* in 1978, are works of subtlety and exceptional artistic character. These qualities are also found in the symbolic decoration of a walking stick from 1975-76 with a squatting female figure and a double-faced head of John the Baptist (12). The seriousness with which Fred still takes this early work is indicated by his remark in the text that the John the Baptist "is a representation to which I would some day like to return..."

A moderate kind of abstraction that is found in all periods of Fred's work is caricature, the distortion of natural form to interpret character. It is prominent in about half the busts and free-standing figures and in all the recent masks. A closely related stylistic device is expressionism, the distortion of natural form to intensify the emotional effect. This is whimsically present in the early grotesques and gargoyles (29-37) but is seriously used in "The Defendant" (60), "Death Mask of a Polish Laborer" (121), and "'Tis in a Strange Bar Late" (143).

The most prevalent abstraction in Fred's work is the wood grain that leaves a pattern of independent lines over the carved detail in even the most realistic pieces. He could have used basswood, which scarcely shows grain, but he has preferred butternut, in which the grain is exceptionally visible. It is, to be sure, in some places used to accentuate form as in "Iowa Hogeyes" (101) and "The Folks" (128), but ultimately it goes its own way. This abstract pattern keeps us constantly mindful of the fact that we are looking at art, which is read as formal relationships, rather than at life.

If Fred were a true realist like the contemporary sculptor Duane Hanson, he would also have to duplicate that most identifying characteristic of natural objects, color. One has the feeling, however, that Fred abhors paint; and his works are inconceivable with it. In this sense he is closer to another modern sculptor, George Segal, who leaves his realistic figures chalk white. What Fred does is actually more innovative than Segal who has behind him the long tradition of sculpture in white marble and alabaster. Realistic creations in strongly grained wood are almost without precedent in art history. Even the medieval sculpture of Germany and the Lowlands that is now in natural oak was, except for that on furniture and architecture, generally painted.

The title of this book classifies Fred's work as sculpture rather than woodcarving. Everything I have said supports that terminology and is consistent with an observation I made about Fred in the Vesterheim exhibition catalogue of 1978: "The young Fred Cogelow is also inclined toward the fine arts, but his love of strong effects give primitive strength to his work." (Henning, Nelson, Welsch. *Norwegian-American Wood Carving of the Upper Midwest*. Decorah, IA: Vesterheim, 1978. p. 20.) The difference between woodcarving and sculpture lies in where objects fall on the scale from craft to art. Most of Fred's work tips that scale in favor of the latter. Neither this nor the fact that he has recently received both the highest rating in sculpture and the People's Choice Award in the Fine Arts Exhibition at the Minnesota State Fair means that he will necessarily be welcomed into the larger world of art. That world rarely embraces, during his lifetime, the man who does his own thing. Fred for sure will do nothing else.

> Marion John Nelson, Director, Vesterheim Norwegian-
> American Museum at Decorah, Iowa and Professor
> of Art History at The University of Minnesota.

Contents

Introduction

Publication of a book like this gives rise to some mixed emotions. On the practical side, the incessant demand for self-promotion and personal glorification make the opportunity nearly impossible to refuse. On the other hand, promotion in which the subject takes a lead role is more than a little suspect. Most troubling, a retrospective glance such as this bears a disturbing resemblance to a post-mortem. ...I pray that, as such, it is premature.

— * —

God only knows why, but it seems like two-thirds of the folks who take an interest in my carvings habitually ask, in the first five minutes of acquaintance, just how it was that I got started in this business. Well, if you'll sit down and make yourself comfortable, I'll tell you.

.. Ass-backwards ... I don't know any other way to describe it. There was always a personal inclination towards art, but it was a largely superficial interest. Then again, when looking back at the omens and coincidences, one wonders if there wasn't a measure of pre-destination at work.

My father, whom I scarcely got to know before he departed this earth, was the proverbial jack-of-all-trades, and likely the master of none. His legacy amounted to a shop of woodworking tools and the dictum that "one's own pain should not be taken too seriously". The shop and a number of the tools were sold off to help make ends meet. The few machines that remained were a perpetual enchantment to me — and nearly killed me a time or two.

Just behind the shop lived old Otto Nygaard and his wife. He was a retired Norwegian chicken farmer and the composer of a number of immemorable piano tunes, including the famous "Well, I Guess I'll Just Have to Go See My Uncle Then!" He was, in addition, a folk-artist who fashioned ornamented jewelry boxes and a number of unusual amusement items. To my brother and me he revealed the secrets of his wood finishes and his unsilvered mirrors — and we forgot the lessons as fast as he gave them. But he left us with an enduring fascination for the feel and smell of wood and an appreciation for the use of detail. The Nygaards were off to the nursing home by the time I was ten. The bitter disappointment of discovering their auction in progress still haunts me.

At the age of twelve I acquired my first set of carving tools. They came in a grab bag which was the reward for having found a new subscriber on my paper route. The tools were cheap soft-steel palm chisels that never did get used. The man who gave them to me said "Say, there you go! Maybe you'll become a famous woodcarver some day." I had my doubts. My Mother had even greater doubts, and actively sought to discourage any such ambitions upon discovering that, in an attempt to make a face with one of my father's palm chisels, I had mutilated her favorite breadboard.

My formal woodworking training was limited to the making of a three piece bookholder in seventh grade. Formal art training consisted of one quarter in both seventh and eighth grades. The teacher found me so precocious that he gave me a special project to complete in the hallway wherein I filled a huge sheet of paper with blotches and then amplified whatever I could see therein. The experiment's results offered no evidence of hidden genius, but pleased the instructor all the same — the class had been so much more enjoyable without me. For the record, it was the first opportunity to catch my color-blindness, and we didn't.

Some years later, while attending the University of Chicago, I signed up for an art class. The Art Department was rather small, consisting of a rather well-known illustrator and a subordinate. While in high school I had ignored the arts, but in college I had again begun to draw with a vengeance. It seemed, after a while, it might be worthwhile to take a drawing course. So I took my assembled drawings to the subordinate to get his recommendations as to the proper course to take. He ranted and raved that I had no back-grounds, and that he could make no evaluations without seeing backgrounds. That cooled my jets for another year, when I signed up for a drawing class from "numero uno".

On the first day of class the the professor strolled in, announced that he was tired of teaching drawing and has decided to change it to a theater class — and the students could design the set, and do the acting, make-up, set-construction, etc. We all just sat there like some namby-pambies and took it. Here we were, not one year out of the rebellious sixties — we of that vaunted radical institution and generation — we just sat on our butts and feigned pleasure with his decision to make a mockery of our contract with him. Perhaps it was Divine Intervention. Perhaps the Almighty did not want my pristine innocence adulterated by this philistine.

I decided to sign up for set design, and thereby get a pointer or two from this fellow one way or another. So I listened to his boring lectures on Greek drama for four weeks, then raised my hand pronto when he solicited volunteers for set design. "No", he said, looking up at me (and I was seated), "You're tall, and we'll use you on construction." It was a little late for dropping that class and taking another, so I took it. Wouldn't have learned anything about drawing anyway, as the set was ultra-modern and consisted of just three plain wall sections and an imitation marble bench. My contribution was an afternoon of putting up pieces of fiberglass sound paneling — for which I received a B+. The reputation of the U. of Chicago fortunately never rested upon its art department.

I never was a luminary presence at that stellar institution anyway. Made a habit of signing up for the classes which required only a six-page paper at the end, and then skipped more classes than I attended. All the same, I learned a lot and benefited greatly from the time spent there. You could be almost dead at that place and still leave a little wiser. There were brilliant minds and scintillating sages, events and people, and architecture — neo-gothic architecture, rich in detail, craftsmanship, and gargoyles.

The original seal of Rural Virtue, Ltd.

My life up to that point consisted of following the path of least resistance. In my junior year of high school I was determined not to return, but family expectations were that I attend college. I fancied West Point, but seeking an appointment seemed like a lot of work. The University of Chicago came to pass only because they came around and stuck money, lots of money, in my face. I never knew what I was doing there, but it sure was fun. Slowly but surely my misgivings about the Vietnam war turned to resolute opposition, and killing time in College seemed preferable to feeding the war machine. When I left the University it was with announced intentions of becoming the manager of the Farmer's Co-op Grain Elevator in Pennock, Minn., knowing full well that the beast did not exist.

Ah yes, Pennock. The home of Rural Virtue and the Font of Human Understanding. It's strange that it was in Chicago that I discovered Rural Virtue. The school was largely made up of Easterners, with a good representation of Chicago area and West Coast residents. In the course of introductions it was the custom of those folks to state only that they were from Framingham or Scarsdale or whatever burb they came from with the understanding that you would know just exactly where that was. But when I countered that I came from Minnesota they'd ask, in bewilderment, just where in Hell that was. So I began to say instead that I was from Pennock. "Ooh,", they'd say, "oh yah.", and pretend to know exactly where outside of Philadelphia or Baltimore that was. It made a wonderful inside joke to those who knew it to be a sleepy little burg of about 400 souls just west of Willmar. It wasn't long before a disenchanted "Westchestercountyite" began to home in on me whenever introductions were being made, just so he could derisively inject, "Oh, don't listen to that — he's from MINNESOTA!" It left me with little recourse but to actively assert the virtues of that bucolic land. And so it was that I began to preach about this rustic little village, nestled picturesquely in the rolling foothills of the mountains of western Minnesota. A town of good Norwegian souls where all but the Mayor lived in humble tarpaper shacks, and he in a grand manse at the top of the hill at the end of Main Street. A community where naught was found wanting; where barefoot children and bovines alike meandered about on the unpaved streets; and where linens were religiously washed and hung out on the line by nine each Monday morning. (It sounded remarkably appealing for a swamp which the railroad had drained so that they could start a prairie settlement of Swedes.)

From college it was home again, and a return to the same old path of least resistance. A cousin's wife observed that I worked well with children (the same level of sophistication and all), and suggested that I consider pre-school education as a career. So I worked for a summer as an aid in the Head Start program, and then continued as a kindergarten aid the following year to get a real feel for the work. God, what misery. It was during that period that I began to work with my hands and to follow the teachings of Reuben Schwartz, the ultimate teacher and guru of Rural Virtue, Ltd. I took a fancy to some horse harness I had seen at an auction and began making horse collar mirrors and a couple styles of chairs of my own design using the hames and lines. I even had a vision wherein ol' Rube assured me that I would go to Sunburg (a Pennock of an even higher plane) when I died if only I collected 500 pair of harness hames.... I did, but I haven't, ...yet.

The period wasn't an entire loss. Acquaintances which later turned into friendships were made with a number of Norwegian and Swedish bachelor farmers. And I began to do a bit of furniture restoration. An expert would not concur with that assessment, but no matter. As luck would have it, one chair had a damaged claw-foot, and carving its replacement was a breeze. That adventure quickly inspired a planter fashioned from a cankerous branch of an oak tree with a face carved in each end. That piece was last seen in the Winona area about fifteen years ago. Presumably it went through a garage sale or two before going up in smoke.

Another year and a half went by before I resumed the effort to manufacture decorator firewood. It was in the middle of a three-year hitch as a counselor to emotionally disturbed adolescents. These kids were difficult for the schools and their parents, but in many cases not nearly so screwy as the latter. The job required taking a week of nightwatch duty every sixth week, during which rounds were made, charting was done, and the wee hours were spent just trying to stay awake. There was a school with a woodshop, and some of the students had been assigned the task of making a woodcarving from a short piece of 2 x 4. One of the blocks was quickly abandoned in the nightwatch office with naught but one corner slightly rounded. The suspicion arose that I could do no worse, and with that reassurance my carving career began.

— ✳ —

Well, sort of. Carving on nightwatch became such a pleasure that in the fall of 1973 I acquired a twelve-piece carving set and a couple of knives, and did some carving during daytime hours as well. I was fast burning out on the job by the spring of '75, so most of each paycheck got put aside for the future. On September 2, 1975, I left the job with intentions of doing a little home repair (re-roofing the house), finishing my epic tale, "The Saga of Suite Lips," travelling for a month, and then woodworking until the money ran out.

When the money finally did run out the following spring my search for employment began, only to end with the realization that I had quite nearly made myself unemployable. My only demonstrable work skills were in a field to which I had no desire to return. My resignation occurred without an eye toward advancement or other employment, and left potential employers suspecting that I was a loser. It likely was of little help that my resumes were crudely typed on poor paper, and that embellishments of my mediocre record were less common than smart-aleck synopses of the truth.

I turned first to cabinetry to eke out a living. (Thank God I was still living with Ma.) Four projects later it occurred to me that I knew virtually nothing about the subject, especially estimating, and I turned more to the carving, hoping to make some sales at art fairs. As a result the next year and a half was spent doing odd carpentry jobs so that I could sell my carvings at or below cost.

In the fall of '77, just after receiving my first "major" commission and after having studied to become a real estate agent, I spotted an ad for a CETA Youth Programs Director for a four-county area. I fervently promised the interviewer that I would give him my devoted services for a minimum of two years if he would but hire me. That didn't impress him but, as luck would have it, he was a bird carver and felt a bond between us. The job and a decent income was mine . . . and I quickly went nuts. In six months the writing was on the wall, and after 11 months the opportunity arose to resign without leaving any of the program participants in the lurch, so I did. A number of commissions were waiting, and the fear that I would nevertheless soon require seasonal or part-time employment proved groundless. I've never looked back.

Early Works
and Cabinetry

Other artists have written and spoken to me of "their vision". After examining their works and now, after looking back upon my own, it is hard to escape the conclusion that an artist's vision is determined as much by that which remains unperceived as it is by that which is seen. It is fortunate, perhaps, that the budding artist is in most cases half-blind, for if he or she were to accurately guage the quality of those first products they would quit at once rather than keep on and invite further humiliation.

The same must be said for this artist (and I use that term loosely). And yet, within many of these early creations there can be found both an innocent charm and a clue of better things to come. Much of the understanding of anatomy appears to have been intuitive, for as the effort to duplicate it became more conscious and academic, some of the initial accuracies succumbed to stiff and errant conceptions of how face and form are constituted.

There are presumably some geniuses or savants, idiotic or otherwise, who can look at something once and immediately see it exactly as it is. For most of us, however, it seems more a case of one perception replacing a previous perception, before it, too, is replaced by succeeding perceptions—each one more accurate than the one before—though correcting one facet often results in diminished accuracy in another. In other words, a perception generally becomes a misconception the instant it is registered, and an artist's "vision" is often simply no more than the point at which he or she decides to look no further. This also accounts for the fact that works executed without a model are often most interesting.

Most of the photographs bearing witness to the dismal quality of many of my early pieces were as bad as the carvings themselves, which relieves us of the pressure to prove the point in this publication. Unfortunately, many of the charming early pieces are likewise lacking a proper photographic record. C'est la vie. A good number of them were executed in bur oak which, once cured, is about as tough and stringy a wood as one can find on this continent. Not too smart for a beginner who didn't know much about sharpening his tools—but it was cheap and readily available. Who should care if it halved my rate of development for those first four years?

If mine is a story worth telling, then the early works deserve some attention, if for no other reason than to provide context and perspective. Some provide hints of promise, and add their own dimension to subsequent works. Others tell stories of directions considered but never taken, while others merely confess to perceptual shortcomings and a lack of sophistication. Most hold some measure of all these traits... perhaps the same holds true today.

Albert the Alligator

"Al" is officially carving number one. There were a couple of pieces — a replacement claw foot and a planter — executed previously with a rotary grinder, but this is the first real carving.

At the time I was a counselor at an adolescent treatment facility and was obliged to work one full week of nightwatch every sixth week. During one such stint, I found a carving project abandoned in the nightwatch office. Some of the students had been given short pieces of pine two by four with the admonition to make something of it, and the frustration level of the individual involved kicked in somewhere about the time that he had one corner slightly rounded.

My personal suspicion was that I could do no worse. The Sunday comics were lying there, including a "Pogo" strip with an illustration of Albert in his li'l putt-putt. So I rendered him on the block, profiled it with the bandsaw in the school's shop, and set at it on subsequent evenings — after charting and between rounds — with a pocketknife and some palm chisels which my father had owned.

Pine, 6-1/2" tall
1973

Man Who Ate Rotten Spaghetti ──

This piece followed Albert in short order.

Behind my father's shop were the stubs of two moving beams, 10 x 10 inch blocks of fir. One was nearly six feet in length, the other about half that. From the time I first started my caretaker role of my father's tools (about the age of nine or ten), I had fancied to one day carve a bust of Alfred E. Neumann — of *MAD Magazine* fame — from one beam and a full-size statue of Alfred from the other.

Following high school graduation I took a five-week college course in the humanities, more to get out of work that summer than anything else. The University of Chicago had given me such a generous scholarship that there was no need to work. When the course ended I returned with noble ambitions of doing Alfred justice, only to find that Ma had given neighbor Einar Berg the large timber, and it was by then neatly split and stacked in his firewood pile.

Fir, 21" high
1974

There wasn't much point in crying over spilt beer. After doing my best to make Ma feel guilty (Norwegian equivalent of money in the bank), I set to work on the smaller block. Two days (and six hours of carving) later, the rendition of the likeness of Alfred consisted of a squarish rise of a nose protruding 3/4" at most beyond two depressions which were to have been the eye areas.

Six years later the project was visited once more, though no longer with the venerable Neumann in mind. God only knows what inspired the expression — the working environment perhaps. The stylized lion heads on the sides came rather directly from an ancient Assyrian design. The completed piece was entered in the crafts competition in the 1974 Minnesota State Fair and received a second or third in the Somewhat Primitive and Awkwardly Charming, Quasi-Functional Carvings Classification.

My appetite for competition was whetted.

Swirlies

Carving Albert was quite a satisfying experience for this noveau carver, and left me rummaging through the basement in search of scraps of wood to duly elaborate. Under one of the benches from my father's shop sat a forgotten box filled with scraps of wood set aside long ago for the next picnic or hot dog roast. Contained within were the remnants of a once fine black walnut table. It had fallen into disrepair and had spent perhaps as much as two decades in the basement awaiting attention before I, in the innocence of youth, decided to clean the basement . . . with an axe.

If it was any consolation, at least it carved nicely. Reckoned it to be from trees from another area, as it was much softer than our indigenous black walnut. That, and the simple pleasure of the activity, made these pieces enjoyable. And while they're unlikely to ever be regarded as high art, they worked to substantially further cultivate my interest.

Untitled
Black Walnut, 8" tall
1974

Lady with Cape and Hat
Black Walnut, 10" tall
1974

Stoic Ambiguity
Black Walnut, 10" tall
1974

Walking Sticks

When it appeared in early 1976 that I might need to sell my carvings at art fairs, walking sticks were among my first productions. Some sold for as little as thirty-five bucks, which hardly made them lucrative, but at least some sold. These two were my very first and were initially priced at $65 and $95 respectively, but were never purchased. That chagrined me at the time, but pleases me now.

The gent was the first, and included the double spiral to give the user something to play with while seated. Simply raising and lowering one's hand with a thumb in one groove and the opposing index finger in the other will cause the cane to twirl. The "Lady's" double spiral is too shallow a grade to work likewise, leaving the user to find other things to play with. That stick was somehow inspired by the John the Baptist story, but why I decided to give him two faces I cannot say, unless for aesthetics. It is a representation to which I would someday like to return for more serious treatment.

Black Walnut, 36" tall
1975-76

Automated Cow

Another early art fair piece which graciously went unsold, perhaps on account of its stiff $30 price tag. Ol' Nell has a simple crankshaft inside her, and as the handle is turned, a pair of udder spigots raise and lower in a complementary fashion. With the fellow's hands firmly

attached, it gives the impression that he is milking her. A cam on the same shaft causes the lower jaw to move with the motion of a chewing cud. Somehow I never remembered to supply a bucket — must have been on account of the milk surplus. Nell is carved from Bur Oak, the man from basswood. The base was made from pine.

Various woods, 10" tall
1976

Half Face

We had a black walnut in our side yard that my mother killed with DDT while trying to rid the tree of caterpillars. Before the tree finally blew over it began to rot on one side. Being of the mind that nothing walnut should be wasted, I took this piece and tried to see what could be done with it.

Smart-aleck sculptors from Michelangelo on (and maybe before) have always quipped that, in carving a bust or an elephant or whatever, they simply removed everything that didn't look like that bust or elephant. . . . in this case, everything too rotten to carve was removed, and a half-face was all that remained.

Black Walnut, 15" tall
1976

Mother and Child

This early relief was taken by some as proof that my sangfroid cynicism was but a veneer; how utterly wrong. It was launched with the idea of concluding as a Mother's Day gift for my dear mom, who at the time was providing room and board with nary a dime in return. Such a present was sure to give her a warm feeling all over and make her forget that she was getting taken. Beyond that, I had just begun chasing Doris and some evidence of finer sensibilities was certain to enhance the prospects for a successful seduction.

Boy, did I ever hit that right. Doris liked the design (from a photo by Nell Dorr, 1971) and the thought that I was planning to do all that for dear old mum so much that she insisted I use some of her late father's lumber for the carving stock. The old man had left a pile of oak out there, and the likelihood was that not much else would ever

Bur Oak, 17" tall x 11" wide
1976

come of it. Or so they said — truth is that there's an ancient Swedish custom which dictates that a man who cuts up another man's lumber is obliged to marry his daughter. . . . live and learn. Straightaway to the barn she dragged me on that frigid February night where, with the aid of a dull handsaw and considerable cursing, we defiled a beautiful eighteen-footer with a cut of which only a caveman could have been proud. Then she ran in to summon the clergy whilst I cleaned up the mess. Fortunately it was so durn cold that night that her message froze in the phone line and, by the time it thawed, her minister of choice had left for a decade's worth of devotion to some missionary position in Africa.

. . . Gosh, this fiction stuff is enjoyable. The truths are that it was her lumber, that I simply liked the picture on which the carving was based, and that I liked it because I'm a sentimental sop. The darn bur oak was so tough that the crooked cutoff was left as was for the top of the piece. Less than 3/4" of the two-inch depth was actually exploited in the carving, but it wasn't the hardness of the material that prompted so much of it to be wasted. It was, rather, my beginner's timidity.

Piano Roll Cabinet

Butternut, 70" tall, 1978
Collection of Bill and Katie
Bernard

In early 1977 the community was deeply shocked when the aspiring magician son of a local attorney goofed and actually had his assistant saw him in half. This appeared to be the final blow to an already shaky marriage, with each spouse blaming the other for having encouraged the departed offspring in his fatal pursuit. Distraught, bereaved, and certain of separation they decided, with the wisdom of Solomon, to cremate the halves of the mortal remains separately, and then draw lots to see who would take which portion. As the year progressed they reconciled but decided that their late son would be humored and honored if his ashes were to find a segregated repose in a two-tier cabinet symbolic of his demise. So it was that this commission came my way.

Gosh, if only the truth were as entertaining....

The purpose for this cabinet was, as the title implies, the warehousing of piano rolls. It was the very sort of work I imagined doing most frequently if woodwork was to be my vocation — a basic piece of cabinetry ornamented with applied carvings. It was, relatively speaking, my first "major" commission, and it didn't take much of a retrospective glance to make me glad that it was the last of its kind. Without any training and a paucity of tools, I was ill prepared — it would have been a short road to ruin. The same commissioner contracted for another seven pieces, and while most were articles of furniture, it was the carving he most appreciated and accordingly, he pushed in that direction; of that I am most grateful.

The Artist as a Young Coatrack ———

Artists are a presumptuous lot. The vocation demands much more than perspiration, a little talent, and simple ego strength. It takes arrogance and gall to presume that others should take their money, which might well be saved or spent on necessary or utilitarian items, and expend it instead on items which are superfluous at best and often unsophisticated and aesthetically lacking . . . and, as a rule of thumb, the money does indeed go elsewhere.

This strikes hard at the artist, who likely remains blind to the deficiencies of his/her work and has been reassured by family and friends that he/she is a budding genius. It strikes especially hard in a society such as this where one's value is often correlated with the income received. The consequences of this contradiction between fancied and realized worth are powerful and often pervasive.

These studies embody the reflection that I might have been of greater value to society as a coatrack. The first study, my favorite, is done in basswood; the second is carved in butternut. The latter is more realistic but lacks the tension and spontaneity, and consequently is not as aesthetically pleasing to me. The detail I most appreciate on the second piece is the self-portrait bust on which the figure rests his hand. The theme retains its appeal, and someday there may be a functional model.

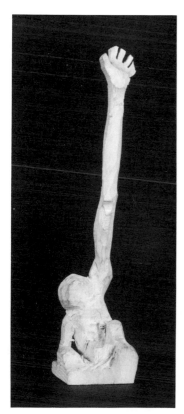

Basswood, 10" tall,
1979

Butternut, 10" tall,
1979

Decadent Bachelor Headboard —————

Doc Hazen was a neighbor who lived just a block away for a good many years before I made his acquaintance. I first encountered him at a bitterly cold auction in November, 1971 when he and his wife outbid me on a rocking chair. It was, to be certain, a "fat Swede rocker," as the sale transpired on Swede Hill and the chair itself was designed to accommodate immense proportions. It was a humongous walnut beauty with its legs, arms and high back formed of one continuous piece — and I lusted after it mightily. When I later reproached him for that calloused act of outbidding me he denied culpability, saying that he had no choice but to follow the demands of his wife.

The dictates of his wife were no longer an excuse when we met again some years later. They had divorced, and in the settlement he had given her the house and lake cottage and had kept the hunting shack for himself. The IRS said his disposal of the other properties constituted a capital gain which obligated him to either pay a lot of taxes or spend a lot of money in upgrading his old hunting shack. His decision was predictable.

My brother Dan did much of the initial remodeling. But he didn't care much for shingling, and asked me if I'd like to make some decent money putting on the cedar. Sort of like asking a German if he'd like a beer.

Now most doctors I have met are afflicted with a profound ambivalence—they don't know whether to consider themselves major or minor gods. In either case they seem ill-disposed towards associating with the likes of you and me except to invade our orifices in search of something that smells of money. So I nearly fell off the roof when Doc came home and, besides crawling up topside and helping with the shingling, actually talked to us as if we were of the same specie.

While we were shingling, Doc expressed an interest in a carved Mexican screen to serve as a headboard. I had no idea what that meant. After thinking it over I gave him an option of either a wildlife scene or an unconventional nude motif for the mural-sized relief I thought he had in mind. He was an avid hunter and outdoorsman, so it came as a bit of a surprise when he opted for the nudes.

The result was the Decadent Bachelor Headboard. The rough design was approved in the fall of '78, with the relief completed and installed the following May. The side statues were completed and set in place a year later. I am unsure as to what conclusion the viewer is to reach from the contrasting demeanor of the two nudes in the relief, and again in the disparity in style of the side statuettes. A sensitive connoisseur of the arts and humanity cannot help but stop and dwell upon that most basic philosophical question of the mortal condition, namely, "Would two women with such different hair-do's naturally be found lying naked together in the same woodlot?"

Relief Mural: Red Elm, 57" tall x 76" wide, 1979
Side Statues: Applewood, 32" tall, 1980
Collection of Dr. Richard Hazen

Doris hated this carving above all other carvings. Probably had something to do with the fact that a blind inebriate might, at twenty paces, have mistaken one of the ladies for her, and consequently feared that some folks might suspect that she did the modeling. The truth is that she had nothing to do with the darn carving except to badmouth it from the start.

This piece was done in red elm, which seemed to be the only species of which I had the correct size and quantity at the time. I knew a bit about the seasonal expansion and contraction of lumber, but chose to pay more attention to the need for expeditious hanging. That being the case, a slightly larger sheet of plywood was screwed to the back of the relief, and its perimeter was then screwed to the wall studs. Toward the edge of the plywood backing the holes were elongated slightly to allow about 3/4" of horizontal expansion and contraction. That wasn't enough. One night the good doctor was awakened by such a loud crack that he first thought someone had shot at him at close range. Jumping out of bed and hitting the lights he perceived a gap of about 1/2" running two-thirds of the way up the right side of the mural. He spent the balance of that night sleeping across the far end of his king-size bed — sleeping, that is, when he wasn't awake thinking bad thoughts of ol' Fred.

After a night or two of sleeping with one eye open Doc decided that he had little cause to fear that the grim reaper would come to him one night in the form of a nude relief. While he wasn't exactly tickled at the huge split in his headboard, he was easy-going enough to let it

ride for another six or seven years, at which time he was remarried and building a mega-addition to his house which included, among other things, a new master bedroom.

The mural, minus the side statues, was moved to the new sleeping quarters. It was removed from the plywood backing, repaired, and set into a bur oak frame where it is free to expand and contract as it darn well pleases; and it does. According to the good Doctor there is over an inch difference in its summer and winter widths in its new setting.

Trumpeting Elephant Table

This is the third of four tables I built and carved for Bill. He had brought the mosaic top home from a trip in Brazil and wanted a table to hold it. The other tables were quite symmetrical, so for this one I thought I'd try more of a free-form design — basically a tree motif. The butterfly mounted on one of the legs was made from a slice taken from a red oak burl.

In the profile view I fancy a broken tusk and a trumpeting elephant's trunk, hence the name.

Black Walnut,
20" tall, 1982
Collection of
Bill Bernard

Rushford Church Doors

Late in 1978 a friend of mine from Winona, a woodturner named Paul Ringwelski, gave me a call and asked me if I'd be interested in doing some carving on some doors for the Rushford Lutheran Church, formerly the Rushford Norwegian Lutheran Church. I told him I wasn't, and that I was too busy in any case. This didn't deter him, as the doors didn't have to be done for six months or so. He explained that the church was preparing for its hundredth anniversary, and that the congregation had a lot of money. So we traveled to that southeastern Minnesota village, nestled in a beautiful valley at the confluence of the Rush and Root rivers, and met with the minister and a church council representative shortly after New Years. There were two sets of double doors in the front of the church that required carving. I suggested that one set of doors be carved to represent the Old Testament and the other to represent the New. The Minister liked this idea, and I agreed to go ahead and design the carvings.

A review of the Old Testament soon had me in a bind. On the face of it, one of the very most important events of that book was God's covenant with Abraham, for it set the Jews apart as His chosen people. The only problem was that He chose circumcision as the sign of that covenant. So I wrote to the fellow I was dealing with and explained to him (didn't take much explaining) the problems of esthetically portraying this in a door panel. "If you'd like, however," I added, "I can make you one hell of a set of door pulls."

The offer was declined, and it was decided instead that the theme be the Church as an institution of both God and Man, with the large

doors devoted to symbolic representation of the life of Christ and the smaller set to His followers. Paul's original intention was to make the doors himself, but while his research provided me with the parameters for their design, it also led him to conclude that he lacked the machinery and experience for their manufacture. A long search eventually led us back to a firm in my home town, the Willmar Sash and Door Co.

Jesus Christ Doors
Red Oak, 94" tall x 35" wide, 1979
Rushford, Minn. American Lutheran Church

Willmar Sash & Door brought the door panels to me as they completed them and I did the carving in an un-used bedroom. On each set of doors there are four large vertical panels, with the symbol on the smaller panel above serving as a summary of the symbols below. The panels of the larger doors start at the bottom and read up, with a dove representing the annunciation, a flower representing Mary, and a star representing the birth of Christ. Above these three symbols is another flower as a symbol of Christ's coming into the world as man. The second panel deals with Christ's teaching, with the symbols of a torch, a lamb and banner, a pair of wings, and the chalice and host representing the last supper. The third panel is headed by a pelican tearing away its own breast. The pelican is a symbol for Christ, coming from an ancient belief that a pelican would, when food was short, tear away its own breast to feed its young. Below the pelican there is a cock representing Peter's denial, a water vessel representing Pontius Pilate's hand-washing, and pair of crossed whips. The last panel deals with the crucifixion and Ascension of Christ and the coming of the Holy Ghost. The other smaller carvings on the doors are of the many crosses and symbols that the Christian Church has used over the ages.

Across the top of the smaller pair of doors there are carved large symbols representing the four Apostles Matthew, Mark, Luke and John. The vertical columns include other symbols representing all twelve apostles.

When the panel carving was complete, they and the doors were taken to Winona for finishing, assembly and installation. It was decided to use the original door frames and to overlay the existing pine trim as the ornate stain glass window above each door was part of an original factory-made unit; new frames would have required their removal and posed considerable risk of breakage. Paul handled the study of and experimentation with bent wood, and then made the forms for bending the curved trim for framing the door and window units. Sixteen-foot oak boards were steamed and bent to the proper shape. The fit was so tight and perfect that only four small finishing nails were used for securing each board.

They never did ask us to return for the dedication, contenting themselves with the presence of a former governor, a good conservative Scandinavian. When asked if they were happy with the results, I've honestly replied, "How should I know, they're Norwegians?" It's like the story of the old Norskie who loved his wife so much that he almost told her.

The Apostle Doors
Red Oak, 94" tall x 29" wide, 1979
Rushford, Minn. American Lutheran Church

Early Works and Cabinetry

Chinese Victorian Coffee Table

One day Bill Bernard asked me to make him a table out of a large hammered brass plate he had brought back from Hong Kong. Long an admirer of Chinese Jade carving, I designed a base with tops reminiscent of that genre and borrowed dragon and flower motifs from the plate for the lower portion. A small caricature of the commissioner crowned each leg and kept the plate in alignment, the consequence of having appreciated similar caricatures worked into the design of pillars at the Yerkes observatory near Lake Geneva, Wis.

This is one of the few pieces for which an exact record of time exists. It took exactly 400 hours from start of the design to completion of the finish. It would likely go much faster today, given increased proficiency and a vastly improved selection of tools — at the time I had less than 20 chisels whereas now some 400 are in easy reach. Then again, today I'd probably add an offsetting amount of refinement.

Black Walnut, 20" tall, 1979
Collection of Bill Bernard

Nude in Pampas Grass ————————

Shortly after my venture into full-time carving Bill asked me for a relatively modest nude. An appropriate model was found in a kitschy little book from my brother-in-law's collection entitled *Youpi and the Girls* by Marcel Veronese.

It was a relatively simple relief, but showed some promise of things to come, particularly in the treatment of the foliage at the top. A partial lamination was made to provide additional depth for the branches. The lamination for the pampas grass, in fact the very inclusion of pampas grass, was made to hide a serious blunder. (I had done the rough-out wasting with a large drill bit, and started by taking the ground out from beneath her feet — a mistake I wasn't the first nor the last novice to make.) All the same, not too bad for a beginner.

Black Walnut, 40" tall x 12" wide, 1978
Collection of Bill Bernard

Sculptor in Wood

Gargoyles and Other Spooky Creatures

Way back in European prehistory folks were a little hard-pressed for entertainment after putting in their 40 hours at the factory. One of the boys, a cross between a chef and an alchemist, cooked up and fermented a potent brew of sassafras roots, elderberry bark and juvenile frog livers. It tasted terrible and smelled worse. Another fellow, on a dare, took a big gulp just to see how long he could hold it in his mouth, only to be bested by another who took a swig and yodeled through it while holding it in his mouth. Before long it was an established rite of passage, and, in time, participants began to swear that the practice freshened their breath and warded off colds. The exercise sounded like an aggressive gurgle, so they called it a gargle—and thus an industry was born.

Unfortunately there were a few in the crowd who couldn't seem to remember to spit it out when they were finished, and they swallowed the stuff instead. Such instances were followed by frightful drunken delusions and vociferous nightmares featuring the strangest of beasties. Witnesses to these occasions came to the logical conclusion that the afflicted were messengers of the gods, and took care to fashion replicas of the creatures described in their delirium with the notion that these icons would frighten away the demons of the night. Not knowing what else to call them they took the name of their drink and called them "gargles". With the passage of time, the term became "Gargoyles".

When Christianity came onto the scene the bishops took a dim view of these grotesque fantasies, and did their best to supplant them. The craftsmen who built the new cathedrals were not convinced of the powers of the new God, however, and decided to hedge their bets by adorning the new houses of worship with representations of their former dieties: two-horned gods, hermaphrodites, biting creatures, bicephalics, and other polymorphs. Conjecture has it that some, like the buxom hermaphrodites, were charms to insure both bounty and virility. Other forms, particularly the grotesques and those prominently displaying their posteriors or genitals, were believed to have the power to drive away evil spirits. (Publisher's Note: This is Fred's version of history — there probably are other versions.)

— * —

My formal education ended at the University of Chicago, a distinguished institution of higher learning, which, in my case, was neither very formal nor distinguished. A lot of wasted opportunities, sad to say. But they should've known better—you can't make a silk purse out of a sow's ear.

Fortunately, much of one's education is incidental and accidental. In the case of this misfit, much of it was tied directly to the physical plant of the University. John D. Rockefeller endowed the school at its start, and they opted to make up for a lack of history by imitating the gothic architecture of more established institutions. The stone and woodwork fascinated me as much, if not more, than the brilliant and sometimes overrated minds which ran rampant through the place. It was a foregone conclusion that some of my first carvings would be of griffins and gargoyles.

Lion Door-Knocker

Eight months after my retirement as a counselor to disturbed adolescents, reality was pounding home the lesson, driving it into my thick skull, that I would either create carvings for sale or have to head back to the stalag. Classical doorknockers had always appealed to me, so it was logically assumed that they would hold that same appeal for others. They — or at least this one — didn't, and most distressingly did nothing to spare me a return to the job of counseling kids. As with the other early pieces that didn't sell, the consequence was a panicky depression, for these were pieces of which I was proud and in which I had invested a fair amount of time — but which could hardly be given away.

Bur Oak, 13" tall, 1976

Such travails yield more than a little touch of madness, and either cripple the "wood-be" artisan or give rise to heightened creativity and tempered perseverance. With time, the retention of those early offerings brings some pleasure and a cognizance of the silver lining to those woes, but for the time when they're up for sale and refuse to sell they are malodorous putrefactive insults to your manhood and dignity.

Though no one thought it worth the $30 or so I was asking for it, I liked it then and continue to enjoy it now. It was one of a number of pieces fashioned from bur oak logs salvaged from an old log home (disguised with siding and an addition) which was knocked down for an expansion of the county fairgrounds. Bur oak gets ever more cantankerous with the passage of time, and a century of drying had left these hunks quite obstinate. That obstinacy, in conjunction with my inexperience, contributed greatly to the bold and primitive lines of the piece.

Two-Horned God Door-Knocker ——

The protruding tongue on this beastie reflects the influence of those gargoyles I first saw at the University of Chicago. This bugger was hacked out of a black walnut limb, most likely from that same yard tree that Ma polished off with the DDT, and it was so hard and obnoxious that it made for blissful reminiscences of working with the bur oak. It was originally stained to even out the difference between the heartwood and the sapwood, but a good many years in the sun and rain pretty much took care of the entire finish, save for a few remnants of the stain which survived to enjoy a new natural-oil finish.

Black Walnut, 18" tall, 1976
Collection of Dr. Richard Hazen

Hinz Gargoyle

Linnea Hinz and I are a long ways from being blood brothers, but both of us are certainly in sync when it comes to enjoying a good gargoyle or two. She wanted one that wasn't too pretty, and this is what she got. I rate it my best early two-horned face. It's not overtly aggressive, yet it has a pleasantly demonic and menacing visage.

Black Walnut, 10" tall, 1980
Collection of Walter & Linnea Hinz

Doris' Door Knocker

For every reaction there is an equal and opposite reaction, and the two months spent working in those holy climes of Rushford and Winona on the Church Door project required a bit of primordial release. So I used a few free evenings to pound out this doorknocker for my sweetie, just to let her know that I was thinking of her during those 80 hour weeks (while she was suffering through an extended jaunt through Ireland with her mother and another lady).

Being in butternut it really isn't heavy or hard enough to be functional as a doorknocker, and I regard it as strictly decorative. The face inside the mouth is intended as a caricature of Doris as she may someday appear as an old woman.

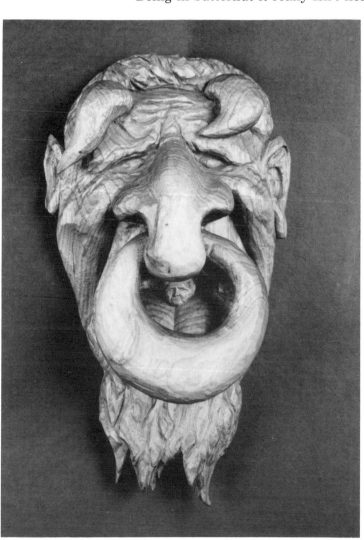

Butternut, 12" tall, 1981

Morning-After Breakfast Companion ————

Sometime in late '84 or early '85 I took a notion to make a memorial to the bar-hopping crowd. The actual impetus was a beautiful windfallen black walnut tree from Alvie Hans' farm — beautiful except for all the barbed wire grown into the bottom four foot section of the tree. The trunk still yielded a ten-foot log 28" in diameter with three clear faces. The four-footer with the wire gave a number of nice slabs before discretion got the better of us and we yanked the remainder off the mill. That remnant measured a little more than 10" x 8" x 4', and would've looked perfect if it weren't for a few chisel and chainsaw surgery scars in the vicinity of four emerging stubs of barbed wire. The ends of the piece were waxed and it was set aside.

When some occasional and haphazard monitoring revealed the beginning of some rather nasty checking (the cracking due to uneven stress in the drying process) it was apparent that the time had come to either use it or lose it. A rough design which would require some lamination to the side was drawn directly on the timber, and a roughout with chainsaw, drill, and chisel commenced. When the piece was far enough along a slab from the same log was bandsawn into shape, and then glued into place with a piece of heavy paper sandwiched in the glue joint. Roughout was continued and several smaller laminations of the same type followed. Once the entire figure was roughed out the assemblage was delaminated. Between the paper and the high moisture content this was no problem. The main block and the first slab were then hollowed as much as possible and stacked off to the side to dry over winter.

The following April they were resurfaced and rejoined. The resurfacing was required by the cupping which drying produces. It's a pain but it goes with the territory. By the end of the month I had a niece's friend posing for the toes at the Swayed Pines Fiddle Festival.

The carving went rather well, all things considered. Northern grown black walnut can be some darn hard stuff, but this particular tree was fairly cooperative. Did run into my hollowing job once on the right side of the face, but was able to cover that error with an applied mole. That was the only applied detail, unless you wish to consider the bar stool which was carved separately.

Aside from a small blue iron stain in the bar stool seat there is no visible sign remaining of the barbed wire which determined the future of this walnut block. If, however, you turn him upside down and shake him you'll hear his brains rattle. That's because all the barbed wire and nails extracted from the block were collected and thrown inside the head when the slabs were rejoined.

— ✳ —

This piece is
pictured in
color on
page 91.

Black Walnut, 53" tall, 1985
#173

This poor bugger is the portrait of a gargoyle suffering from alcoholic excess and sleep deprivation. Fatigued and impotent by the early light of dawn he's got the morning blues and ain't hardly got the energy to quaff his stale beer, much less drive away your evil spirits or conjure up a few of his own. He just wants to sit there quietly, across the breakfast table from you, hoping to borrow some occasional attention — thinking that maybe you'll look into those sad brown eyes and realize that he's just another suffering being on this old planet earth.

Much as each of us would fancy ourselves to be unique, we tend to use ourselves as the standard for the norm. Indeed such is often the case with this writer. There wasn't any doubt in my mind that this piece was great, and that some soul of moderate affluence would soon claim him as his/her personal morning companion. I was wrong. But that was all right, as I had been in need of a personal gargoyle myself.

It must be confessed that he was intended to be somewhat offensive to prudish sorts — he apparently succeeded a bit too well.

I can easily think of another eight gargoyles that I have carved along the line — which means there's probably at least a dozen. When the scholars talk about gargoyles they generally include

grotesques, and I shudder to imagine what percentage of my work might fit that description. But carving these beasts is, as with caricaturization, a special pleasure. Freedom from realism is the freedom of spontaneity — the freedom to carve intuitively and almost purely for the joy of carving. It is the singular enjoyment of running the steel edge through the wood.

I can imagine carnal pleasures which easily surpass the joy of carving "on automatic", but cannot imagine enjoying those pleasures for as long, or as often, as carving — and still find them enjoyable. Someone once said "What's eternal bliss like after awhile?" I'm not sure I'd want to unceasingly carve my way through eternity, but I can think of worse fates.

Hazen Gargoyle

Doc Hazen added onto that old hunting shack so many times that I have trouble recalling which carvings correspond to which addition. On one of these additions he enclosed the backside of his huge brick fireplace so as to have his main entry and a relapsing room right behind it (the fireplace). The entry hall was two stories in height, and ran into a second-floor balcony opposite the front door. The back of the fireplace was a good seven feet in width, protruded a couple of feet into the hall, and began its taper to the chimney about nine feet above the floor. All that brick seemed to demand a gargoyle for its own—one to glare down upon each and every entrant. The good doctor was one of the very few with an ear attuned to these cries of the brick.

With all the mammary ensconced in the bedroom (the headboard, page 18) it was only right to balance the house with some more of the same on the other end. So I conjured up an original hermaphroditic polymorph to meet any conceivable traditional guideline: a fox-tailed, male dog hind-quartered, buxom, warty-handed, tongue-protruding antlered gargoyle custom built to cling to the stepped masonry.

Honduras Mahogany, 20" high x 20" wide x 40" deep, 1980
Collection of Dr. Richard Hazen

Figures in the Round

If I was to write a general overview of large "in the round" woodcarvings, the dissertation might be subtitled: "A running battle with the totem pole." It likely has a great deal to do with the medium, particularly its natural form of presentation, and often the greatest problem in carving these figures — especially from a limb or from a log — is to create a product which comes across as something more than a decorated fencepost.

It is a task that sounds easier than it is. The flow of line and form must be esthetic and pleasing, and yet must conform to rather rigid parameters governing any augmentations to the log (such as shrinkage, structural soundness, and other factors). The headaches are such that a carver will often wish he worked in clay or in bronze, where he can simply glop on more goo or weld on another hunk of metal. In the end, however, it is that special character of wood — the ineffable something that gives life to the work — which makes it all worthwhile.

Dog Dies Running

The period of 1982-83 was notable for the number of key changes in my life and career. July, '82 saw the beginning of studio construction, a twenty-seven month project which was to cost very little thanks to the quantity of available salvaged and recycled materials. These savings were unfortunately offset by a tripling or quadrupling of the time involved in construction, but the freedom it brought me from my basement internment was to make it all worthwhile. Despite the time drain from construction and an ingrained addiction to logging dating back from '76, the years were productive ones, bringing new directions and new levels of comprehension and finesse. These years also saw my entry into carving competitions, in which my success was soon to make me a household name within a four-block area.

This piece figured heavily into that equation, but its greatest contribution to my career was tangential, if not extraneous, to the piece itself. This piece marked, more than any other, an emancipation of both the artist and his spirit. It was the sculpture which led me to believe in myself, and in the value (relatively speaking, of course) of my works. It marked the point at which I could honestly feel I had a right to fair compensation, as opposed to the condescending patronage which sustained a panderer of frivolities.

That's not to say I thought it was on a par with cousin Michelangelo's "David". For the most part, it's simply a manifestation of a childhood fascination with the romance of the noble warrior, executed with a bit of artistic license. It's chief strength is its mastery of the fragile details (Dog Dies was carved entirely from the one original block of wood) and in its incipient awareness of nuance. And that, for the time, was enough.

His attire is much the same as that of the following piece, "Hunts the Crying Bear", save that his headpiece is adorned with the head of a red-tailed hawk. Buffalo horns with the compound curves, such as those installed on both of these headdresses, are said to occur, but only most infrequently — unless, of course, you are an artist in search of a little extra class.

*Butternut, 24" tall, 1982
Collection of Joe Thompson*

Hunts the Crying Bear

Hunts the Crying Bear depicts a fictitious Oglala chieftain looking out over the Thieves' Trail about 1874. The Thieves' Trail was the first road that prospectors cut into the Black Hills of South Dakota following the Custer Expedition's discovery of gold there in August, 1874. He holds a ceremonial lance adorned with eagle feathers and the head of a golden eagle. His headdress sports the head of a black-footed ferret and seven more eagle feathers. The buffalo fur for the headdress was taken from the hump of the animal, then cut and sewn to the desired fit before the horns were attached. The tassels were made from strips of ermine fur.

Hunts Bear's shield was made from shrunken buffalo hide. It contains a simple quilled pattern plus painted bear claws and tears reflecting the vision from which he took his name. Three of the shield's five feathers are attached to a stick and then attached to the shield. The foot of a golden eagle is also attached for its particular medicine.

He wears a bear claw necklace with an eagle bone war whistle attached. His bone and bead breastplate is trimmed with scalp locks. The pouch tied to his breastplate would have contained something relevant to his personal "medicine"—a sacred stone, a piece of fur or hair, an animal tooth, etc. His own braids were wrapped with a double helix of tradecloth. The brass wristband was either taken in trade or removed from the body of a foe. Each of his leggings were made from one whole skin of deer or antelope fringed with scalp locks.

His attire is basically true to the period, except that his leggings would have been replaced by straighter cuts and tradecloth material by that time, and he almost certainly would have been wearing a "medicine shirt" when sporting the shield and headdress. Artistic license was invoked to allow for those deviations.

This was, in many respects, the most difficult piece I've carved to date, and, I would venture, about as demanding as anything you'll find being carved these days. It was made from a single block of laminated 2" butternut and mounted on a separate base rendered from a log. Carving a piece such as this from one block of wood poses incessant problems of accessibility, fragility, and orientation. The inclusion of any realistic wind-blown appendage requires that the point to which it is affixed must be rather closely determined before the appended detail can be defined. In other words, the body and spear have to be carved first, which means you must carve around and behind numerous over-sized blocks left as "protected areas" to be later carved into feathers, locks, a pouch, wristband, etc. Further, as these blocks are gradually formed into the particular detail, "bridges" must be left connecting these feathers, locks, etc. to each other and to the body to protect them from breakage. These problems would not have been so great if some of the details had been later applied or inserted, or if the piece had been sculpted first in clay and then duplicated in wood. As it was, only about 3/4 of the originally planned detail survived. It was simply too difficult to determine sufficient points of reference with all the protected areas in the way.

With the scope of my ambitions diminished the rate of progress improved dramatically---to something akin to the speed of a glacier. At that time I had only about 40 chisels and a few knives and dental picks, compared to about 10 times that amount at the present time. (Most of the 400 chisels and 30 dental picks collect dust but for a few days a year. But when that "one tool" alone does the job in 30 seconds, rather than 20 minutes with the best alternative, it doesn't take long to justify a sizeable collection.)

Dr. Pat Malone ordered Hunts Bear after failing to acquire my

Butternut, 42" tall, 1983
Collection of Dr & Mrs. Pat Malone
#157

first Indian. He treated me much more than fairly. My fantasy is to become filthy rich so as to afford sending him and his wife to Paris for a week or two at my expense as a token of my appreciation—but alas, it hasn't happened. It would be more realistic to anticipate a gratis tour of Sunburg with lunch at the local cafe.

Hunts the Crying Bear quenched, if not suffocated, any further desire to create fictitious Indians of the western romance genre. It's all well and good to prove that you can throw in all sorts of trappings just to make life difficult for yourself, and to do a number of them in near impossible situations. But that's not the same as capturing the spirit of an individual.

This piece is pictured in color on page 90.

Kilroy Was Here Too

Subtitled: "A Lament for Gary Hart, Jim Bakker and Fred Cogelow" or "It's a Woman's World, Baby."

In the spring of '87 the remnant of Alvie's nail-infested walnut beckoned, saying it contained a cool, nude lady. The goal was to do a

woman for whom the average man would tear off half of his unessential appendages while she just sat there totally oblivious to the notion that she could be of any interest to anyone.

There is a special challenge in carving a nude. One forgets until it's too late how damnably bothersome it is to think of nothing but beautiful naked women when there isn't even a compliant one around.

It was one of those endeavors where my model in the mirror was of no help whatever. I would have attempted to procure a live model, which is what a feller using my approach really needs for any human figure, but that wouldn't have worked at all. My constitution is such that trying to carve in the presence of a naked woman would drive me nuts, on top of which a jealous wife would likely be prone to do some detrimental remodeling of my cranium, if not some parts of even greater value. Doris is all for artists using naked models, so long as they're other artists. Of course, if the shoe were on the other foot you'd never find me objecting....

Black Walnut, 21"tall, 1987
#209

Leavin' in Style

You'd have to be quite perverse or more than a little obtuse to grow up in these parts and be immune to the influence of the western artists Russell and Remington. Early in '84 they subliminally urged me to take on this mildly complicated rodeo figure.

A fellow named Fred Schnell wrote a book back in '71 called *Rodeo, the Suicide Circuit,* and it included one particular photograph that caught my eye. The photo showed an old bronc buster about to greet the old terra-firma in a most ungainly manner. I've always liked horses but have never been overly familiar with them (did call several I've met by their first names, but that was because they didn't have any known surnames), so I first tried a basswood prototype to see if the idea looked feasible. It did, despite a torso on the horse that came out about 25% longer than it should have.

I drew up a modified profile from the photo, cut the appropriate silhouettes out of 2" black walnut, and laminated up the block. After that it was just a matter of proceeding from what is known to what is suspected and deemed highly probable, with numerous consultation trips to my brother's collection of *Western Horseman* magazines.

The cowboy was a bit easier than the horse. I tied a belt to a doorknob and prevailed on a couple of neighbor kids to take turns pretending to fall off a wooden crate, which they would have done had they not been firmly grasping onto the belt. With the youth of today not being quite so compliant and readily available as I would like, I had to spend a good bit of time falling off the crate myself while looking in a mirror to get things figured out.

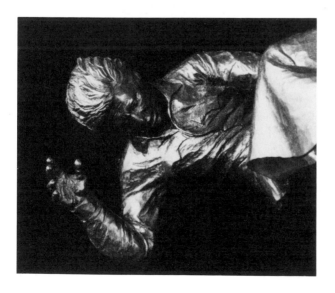

This is quite a fragile piece. Some walnut is harder than other walnut, and this stuff was like a rock when carving across the end grain, which makes its fragility all the more impressive. The cowboy is held to the horse where his behind touches the flank strap, an area a bit smaller than the diameter of an ordinary pencil. It is the man's fingers of which I am most proud, however, as they are all quite small and delicate, some running entirely cross-grain, yet all were carved, including fingernails, without breakage.

Black Walnut, 12" tall, 1984
Collection of Ray Waechter
#166

Figures in the Round

Waitin' to Swing

There is a pressure on artists who depict American Indians to show them as romantic figures of the Wild West. As appealing as that might be, there comes a time when one would prefer to show them as individuals, as shallow and as complex as the rest of us.

Much of my own shallow complexity relates to the contemplation of death. This may be due to the childhood loss of my own father, or perhaps because of the audacious people who have suggested that it might well be my own eventual fate. But it's one thing to contemplate death as something coming in its own due time and quite another to fathom the thoughts of those who, in their prime, await execution and a particular date of termination.

This work was inspired by, and liberally adapted from, a photo of Chief Shakopee found in the Minnesota Historical Society's archives. Chief Shakopee was the third Mdewankton Sioux Chieftain by that name. He gained his place in history during the central Minnesota Sioux uprising of 1862. This was, though brief, the most bloody of the western Indian wars. It erupted in consequence of the usual factors— treaty violations, unscrupulous trading practices, etc; but it was, in essence, the poignant story of a people caught between two cultures. In this case the "Long Hairs", or "Blanket Indians", rebelled and took vengeance on both white settlers and on the "Short Hairs"—those Indians attempting the change from a nomadic to an agrarian existence. The uprising was not just caused by hunger and a desire for freedom; it was a desperate and final quest for dignity and manhood in accordance with the precepts of a warrior culture.

Some 303 warriors were sentenced to hang for their participation in the outbreak. President Lincoln commuted the sentences of all but 39. Of those, 38 were hanged in Mankato in December, 1862. Chiefs Little Crow, Shakopee, and Medicine Bottle escaped with their small bands to the Dakotas and

Original photo of Chief Shakopee which inspired "Waitin' to Swing" carving.

Butternut, 22"
tall, 1985
Collection of
McDonalds of
Canada
#181

then into Canada. Little Crow returned to steal horses and was killed near Hutchinson in June, 1863. In December, 1863, the other chiefs were located in Canada, and in mid-January they were drugged and smuggled back into the United States by dogsled. In a trial not noted for its exemplary judicature, Chief Shakopee was convicted of many of the most horrendous atrocities of the war and sentenced to hang, along with Medicine Bottle. In the absence of direct evidence, their convictions were based largely upon the boasting they had done during internment. The sentence was not carried out until November 11, 1865. In the meantime the pair served as both trophies and entertainment — savages put on exhibition for the ladies and gentlemen from St. Paul and other nearby communities. It is recorded that Shakopee "made a favorable impression as he was intelligent and told interesting stories."*

The historical photograph shows the Chief wrapped in a threadbare blanket with a kerchief wrapped around his head. His locks were shorn and his clothes were those of the enemy. He was not posed, but certainly complied with the wishes of the photographer. The ultimate irony was that he, like many of the 38 hung before him at Mankato, may have accepted the white man's God in his final months of captivity. For the carving I removed a prop beneath his left elbow to make the piece a bit more self-contained. The restoration of his braids and Indian garments made him more identifiable as an Indian and a better symbol of the values and cause for which he was about to die.

* *A Disgraceful Proceeding — Intrigue in the Red River Country in 1864,* by Alan R. Woolworth, Minnesota State Historical Society, 1963.

Familiarity Breeds Contempt

From one of the first butternut trees I ever harvested there came an exceptional "banana", a four-foot log of a banana shape, with a markedly off-center pith. Running such a log through the mill results in phenomenal waste, whereas the simple elimination of the pith during carving yields a fairly stable hunk of wood. The log was set aside to dry intact for some years, waiting for its special fate.

Sometime in '84 I began to take notice of my nephew Kent, a charming little 2-1/2-year-old at the time. Not having any children of my own, and rather dreading the possibility, my proclivities were instead directed towards trees, women, trucks, and saws. But these partialities notwithstanding, it one day dawned on me that here was this cute little fellow and a darn good potential subject for a carving. He was also an uncooperative subject. Numerous camera studies proved worthless. Then I noticed him standing in the background of a haphazard, perhaps even accidental, shot taken at a Christmas gathering. It wasn't much from which to work, but it did provide an attitude and posture.

Kent had his feisty moments at the time, and his stance seemed incomplete. So I borrowed a pinnochio toy and placed it in his grasp, upside down. Such was the genesis of one of my ambiguous titles, "Familiarity Breeds Contempt". The viewer is left to decide whether it is the child's familiarity with the toy or an adult's familiarity with

the child which engenders the disrespect. (I understand that Kent's mother did not find the title amusing.)

Children are difficult subjects, especially for someone like me who has had minimum contacts with them. Perhaps most gratifying was the fact that Kent was quite enamored of the carving from the time he first saw it, and was given to reach out to hold its free hand.

Butternut, 36" tall, 1985
Collection of David and Jane Binger
#176

Ed — Stearns County Farmer

In the spring of '86 the muse of inspiration strongly suggested a life-size figure of a farmer planting potatoes. There is an inherent desire to treat The Voice as Divine Intervention, though it more often turns out to be something that was growing on that old cheese you used on your noon sandwich. The intimation was on the verge of attribution to the latter when one day, right there before me in the breakfast food aisle of the local Cash-Wise supermarket, stood that perfect potato farmer model. Alas, the flesh is weak. While I'm ordinarily a bit of a nervy guy, I could not bring myself to then and there invade his privacy. But when, moments later, I again beheld him in all of his bucolic glory in the frozen food section, trying to decide between a box of fudgcicles and half-gallon of ice cream, it became undeniably clear that this indeed was the hand of God at work.

. . . He was not at all convinced. He opined that you'd have to be sick to want a statue of a homely old cuss like himself, and the mention of the fact that I paid my models didn't seem to interest him in the least. I backed off and turned to small talk. Learned that his name was Duscher, uncle to a boy I worked with as a kindergarten aid some 14 years previously. As we took to discussing weather conditions and crops he began to warm up. When he finally asked, "How much do you pay?" I knew he was hooked.

A photo session quickly followed. After developing the film I quickly laid to rest the idea of planting a spud planter. So he got another visit and we took another bunch of photos, including a few of a very relaxed farmer leaning against the wall with his can of beer.

— ✳ —

The number one problem in working with a big log is "checking"— the cracking of the wood as it shrinks from drying. Checking occurs as the wood seeks to accommodate the stresses that result from uneven drying. The easiest way to diminish checking is to rough-out the log as rapidly as possible and then make a chainsaw cut, or kerf, along the backside. This kerf cut runs the length of the log and extends to the pith or center of the log. This cut will alleviate tension by opening as the wood shrinks, thereby reducing or eliminating the checking that would otherwise occur elsewhere. The expanded kerf must later be filled with a spline, of course.

The other alternative (aside from certain chemical treatments) is to hollow out the log. With its center removed the pressures are more uniform and checking on the outside is reduced or eliminated. The problem with this method is that it is a laborious and risky process, as it is easy to hollow out too much. The advantage (over the kerf cut method) is that you are not left with large and unsightly disruptions in the grain pattern.

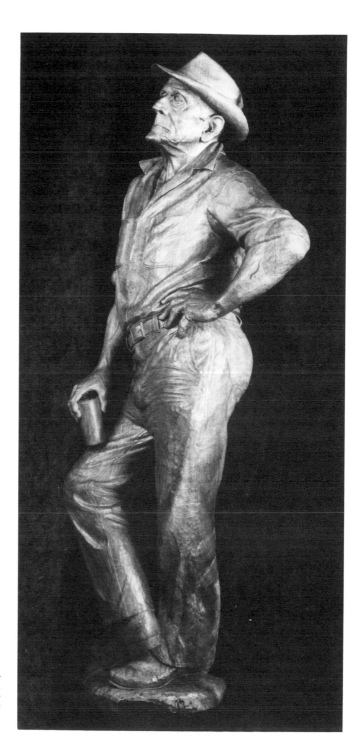

Silver Maple
72" tall
1986
#195.

Ed was hollowed out from the arm that leans against the wall and from the top of his head. A couple of l-1/4" holes were drilled through his hat and several radiating holes were established from these, starting an inch or so beneath the surface. Chiseling and mashing followed, and four final entrances were established through the ears and nostrils. The chest was hollowed out from the hole in the right arm with a chainsaw, followed by whatever manner of drills, bits, and other tools that could be introduced through that window of opportunity. The log had decayed a bit too much in the vicinity of his left elbow and required a transplant. This provided an opportunity to drill up the forearm and his upper arm into his shoulder where it joined with holes coming from the chest cavity.

The side and top openings were later sealed. The right arm with a plywood cover and a felt facade and the top (hat) with a wood plug with grain matching the surrounding wood.

Working on a rapidly drying log is an exciting process. Your control is limited and you have no absolute way of predicting what will hap-

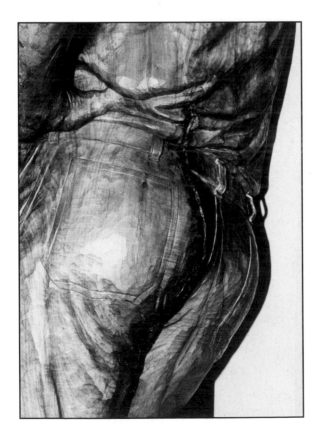

pen. It is a race against time trying to remove as much wood as possible, as fast as possible, both inside and outside. The eyes are usually the last thing I carve, but I pencil them in early to enhance the character and feel of the piece. With Ed I'd get the eyes about as I'd like them, carve on another part for a day or two, then realize that his eyes had moved another eighth of an inch closer and now looked screwy. The shrinkage is quite significant. During the initial carving a check opened in the left side of his hat brim, and eventually reached a width in excess of 1/4". But by the time his head had been hollowed out and had stopped shrinking, this check had closed up absolutely tight.

— ✳ —

The correct title on this piece is "Stearns County Farmer—milks cows and drinks beer". Stearns County is a lot like Wisconsin, full of beer-drinking

Figures in the Round

German Catholic dairy farmers. The main difference, according to the generally reliable Kandiyohi County Lutherans United for the Defamation of Papists, is that Stearns County farmers are alleged to have a history of extensive inter-family marriage — so extensive that they are on the verge of creating a distinct sub-species. So far this phenomenon has been tactfully referred to as the "Stearns' County Syndrome".

In my youth I always thought of it as the "SinDrome", and had fantasies of visiting the place. Kandiyohi, the county of my home and my birth, was a dry county from the time of prohibition or before, so it was the custom of juveniles of my area to head 20 miles north to St. Martin, St. Stephen, El Rosa, or any of the other good Catholic towns to get beer, providing they were tall enough to see over the counter. Now, to the average American, the consumption of beer is no big deal, but to the righteous teetotaling Norskies of Kandiyohi County the mere thought of beer was a bigger sin than lusting after your neighbor's wife — or cow.

So, with the real Ed living just three miles south of that nefarious land of alcohol, I couldn't resist the chance to let the title reflect on the moral inculcations of my youth. The irony is that Ed can't stand alcohol, even though he is of German descent. The beer can was available only because a son would keep some around for his occasional stop-by.

The Real Ed Duscher and my representation.

The Defendant, Soon to be Hanged, Addresses the Jury

Subtitled: John Brown

This work, in many respects, is the complement to "Waitin' to Swing" (p. 48). This historical fantasy of that colorful and complex man was inspired by the painting done of him and hanging in the Kansas Statehouse, in conjunction with those same factors which inspired the portrait of Chief Shakopee. There are a number of parallels: each fought with determination for that in which they believed, and each, when his fate was sealed, faced it with dignity and civility. The difference was that John Brown was a zealot, and it is for this reason that it actually disappoints me somewhat that in his final days he gained acclaim for his courtroom grace and propriety.

What place do the laws and courts have in the eyes of one who takes the lives of noncombatants in a holy war, as John Brown is suspected of doing in the pro- and anti-slavery battles in the Kansas Territory? What deference can and should they demand when God is on their side? It is my preference to imagine this fiery infidel towering over a front-row juror, spewing forth a vitriolic stream of vehement and righteous indignation at the inequities and abominations of the system which he, the juror, sits to protect.

— ❋ —

The innovative feature of this carving is that the head is actually a mask. The statue is intended to stand upon a four-foot high pedestal, so that the viewer catches the full effect of the anger, with a "flash" of light coming through John's eyes, nostrils, and mouth.

Basswood, 48" tall, 1987
#210
Tinted Lacquer Finish

Figures in the Round   **61**

The Story's About Joe's Wife

My conscious attempt for some time now has been to render figures in a more everyday manner — ordinary folks doing ordinary things. When we remodeled our house we had a Norwegian carpenter install the kitchen cabinets. This meant that the work was done well, but very, very slowly. In keeping with the finest of Nordic traditions the fellow was exceedingly fond of his coffee breaks. As my brother, the chief carpenter on the project, was similarly inclined, these intermissions were appropriately stretched to accommodate whatever jokes, gossip, and bits of trivia needed to pass the lips of the motley crew assembled.

As I watched this fine Scandinavian specimen as he perched with easy grace upon a bar stool, his eyes lighting at the tantalizing tidbit offered as introduction to the latest story of someone else's misfortune, the sculpturesque qualities of his pose flashed like a neon light. Were it in my power he would have been turned into stone and frozen in that instant. Instead I asked him to hold it while a camera was located. He obliged, but in typical self-conscious fashion he altered both his position and expression. I took the photos anyway to flatter him, and they were quickly misplaced. But the idea lingered in the fetid recesses of my mind.

So it was later that I started the piece, using some sketches made of my mirror model. As the piece progressed, the stupidity of pursuing it with neither photos nor actual model became manifest.

* * * *

Of the conversation in progress we know nothing, save that the indiscretions of Joe's wife about to be described would be somewhat less amusing if they had been committed by the storyteller's wife.

Sketch made of myself while viewing one mirror through another mirror.

Sculptor in Wood

This piece is
pictured in
color on
page 89.

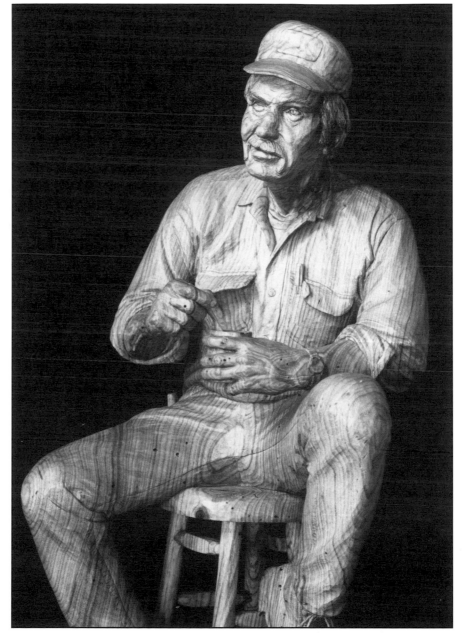

Butternut, 30" tall, 1990
Collection of
John F. McMillen
#256

"Gust" — With Thoughts of Mabel

Paynesville is another of the small, mostly German-Catholic towns that dot the western part of Stearns County. It's home to the finest saddle shops between Minneapolis and Fargo and a couple of the finest little ma-and-pa restaurants you'll find anywhere. Doris and I make it a point to stop in and sample the cuisine at Tuck's whenever we come through town.

It was late in '88, with thoughts of a summer of major exhibitions weighing on my mind, that we happened to pass some time there. It was a time of year when the old farmers don't find a lot to do between milkings except to go to town for some coffee. Well, it's right hard for me to sit and watch old German farmers shuffling in and out, getting coats on and off and gumming their egg sandwiches while shooting the breeze without getting powerfully inspired — especially since I had just harvested a long-dead butternut tree the previous fall and had saved the 20+" butt log for a life-sized sculpture.

Within a couple of days I had talked a retired neighbor into putting on his bib overalls and contorting himself in this way and that for the better part of an hour while I did some photo studies. The ideas weren't bad, and the model was unusually adept for a first-timer, but the postures were too expansive for the log and the execution a bit too demanding for the time frame I had in mind.

The idea went on the backburner for a couple of months. Then one day a photo article on Missouri in the National Geographic caught my eye. There was a photo taken by Veronica S. Morrison of an old farmer walking back to his barn carrying an empty cream can. It was a rear view, with a bit of the old boy obscured by a second cream can. It gave the impression that the feller knew the photographer was there, and had abandoned the second can halfway down the drive-way to expedite his retreat. The posture was perfect — but the detail left

This piece is pictured in color on page 87.

Butternut, 72" tall, 1990
Collection of Ella
Carothers Dunnegan
Gallery of Art,
Bolivar, Mo.
#259

something to be desired. So I called an old farmer who lived halfway between Pennock and Sunburg who had been recommended to me as a potential model and asked him to pose.

Whatever happened to the good old days when peasants looked like peasants? When they wore ragged, threadbare clothing to nicely complement their look of perpetual fatigue. This feller was pushing 80 years old but didn't look a day over 50, and he wasn't much fatigued. And his bib overalls looked like something his wife had pressed and set out for church on Sunday. I asked him to wear the look of exhaustion, and he said he was doing his best but that the darn can just didn't weigh enough empty to make it look like any effort. So we filled the can with rocks, but it still looked like he was hauling a feather pillow.

Had it been the good old days when peasants were peasants I would have grabbed an axe handle and beaten him roundly about the shins and back until he crumpled to the ground. Then he could have been revived and postured properly. Maybe after a few more years of "Bushy-Reaganism" those good old days will return, but in April, '89, I had little recourse but to try again. However the weather turned cold and my models were disinclined to stand around in the cold and damp with a cream can filled with rocks in hand. So I decided to go ahead on just the basis of the National Geographic photo. . . .What a mistake!

That isn't to say that I started right in on the log. First came a series of 3-1/2" high figures based solely on the interpretation of the magazine photo. The third of these figures looked sufficiently engaging to warrant a life-size profile, so a rear profile was drawn up. Actually it was 10% over life-size, but that seemed to defeat the objective of having the figure look tired and worn, so it was reduced to life-size. Then the log was attacked with the old chainsaw.

The size reduction was fortunate, as the log was still too small for the project. It was not the decisive attack it should have been. The challenge in woodcarving is not the detailing — it's figuring out where the darn details go in the first place. If you're working on a small piece it is a small matter to leave that extra percentage of wood in the roughout to accommodate any shifting of the particulars as the carving progresses. As the work becomes larger the effort in such an approach increases at nearly an exponential

Study for "Gust"

rate. And when you compound the problem with less than adequate knowledge of the subject and the need to carve on imaginary extensions you're navigating in uncharted waters.

The tree may have stood there dead for six years, but it was still full of free water, which necessitated internal surgery. Hollowing out the face wasn't hard, as only its back half was in the original log. A basswood block had been applied to the front of the head until the roughout was completed — and then removed and replaced by the best match I could find in butternut. The final face was held in place with three dowels and a band clamp until it was nearly complete, and then hollowed out to make a mask which was then glued to the (also hollowed-out) back of the head.

Hollowing out the chest cavity was a good deal more troublesome. The size of the log required that the arms would have to be attached, but not at the shoulder. The right arm joint allowed for a chainsaw and long-bit drill entry, and this hole eventually allowed entry to the forearm with palm chisels and a scorp. Large holes were also drilled down from the inside of the head into the chest cavity. By the time the cursing had faded Gust was pretty well hollow from the top of his head to the bottom of his chest pockets, with a number of holes extending much deeper.

The hollowing was, of course, a risky business. Yet it had to be done to accelerate drying, reduce checking, promote final stability, and to improve quality glue joints.

— ✳ —

A piece like Gust is undertaken with the understanding that it won't be anywhere close to perfect. With four different body models (varying in height by at least a foot and in weight by 70 pounds or more), five separate bib overalls, and three different shirt models the result could've looked like Frankenstein. Proceeding from what is known, to the safe bets, to the good hunches, you are gradually taken over by the commitments made in error. Then a period of seemingly interminable fudging sets in. This graciously ends one day when you tell yourself, "This is what I've done and I have to live with it. But that's OK, cause, by God, I like his attitude. Once the details are in not 1 in 500 will notice the liberties taken anyway."

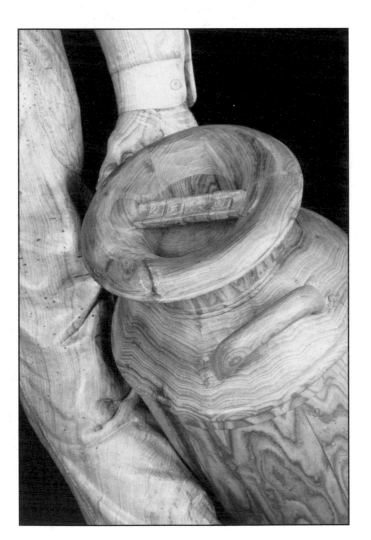

That's kind of where it ends. I like old Gust, (a name he acquired not as a nickname for Gustavus, but by virtue of a youthful proclivity towards fragrant zephyrs). His neck is perhaps a bit overdone on the hyperextension, but it and his forward lean are a nice counterpoint to the weight of his burden. The pocketed hand tells you he's been there before. With the far-off look in his eye you can't be sure if his mind is on the markets or on Mabel, or if Mabel is his wife or a cow — or a cow he named after his wife.

Caricatures

Caricatures are a great place to start a sculpting career — and, I suspect, quite likely a good place to end one. There is considerable freedom from the rigorous parameters of realism, yet the success of the individual endeavors demands an eye to realistic elements and nuance. The mimicry and exaggeration — the license and opportunities — lend themselves to a more relaxed and more rapid development, and the humor makes it all the more enjoyable.

My caricatures tend to be a bit more involved and sculpturesque than the norm, perhaps due to the fact that they're sculpted rather than whittled.

It's a Man's World, Honey ─────────

Adolph Highstrom, my old sawmill and woodlot accomplice, saw fit to begin the year 1980 with a stroke, and at the age of 83 found himself residing in a nursing home. In late April of that year he accompanied us to the Swayed Pines Fiddle Festival and spent the day showing off his new wheels and entertaining the crowds. While he sat chit-chatting with the ladies I did my darndest to sculpt a bust of him out of a butternut log.

Some two weeks later a cerebral aneurysm finished him off, and I resolved to take a suitable marble slab which we had in our basement and carve in it an appropriate epitaph to set below his headstone. "Here lies the man who crowed" was the only inscription that seemed to fit. He always had been a cocky little bantam rooster of a guy, vying for the attention of the ladies and bragging about his way with them — even though he was a life-long bachelor. Neither was he shy about advertising his smarts, nor was he hesitant to take a swing at someone twice his size, even into his late 70's. He even boasted that his Christianity was far better than anyone else's. To top it off, if he became bored with your conversation or if he simply wanted some attention, he'd put his head back and crow like a rooster. And indeed that he did do well enough to brag about.

Swedish Defiance
Butternut, 24" tall, 1984
Collection of Mary Thein

About the time the epitaph was finished it occurred to me that he and his brothers hadn't bothered to procure a headstone for either the sister nor their father, and that Adolph's brothers were likely to continue that family tradition, even though his estate would easily have covered the cost of a small mausoleum. Following a brief consultation with one of the brothers Adolph's name and dates were entered on the reverse side of the marble slab, and with the brother's help it was soon erected at the gravesite. Some weeks later, miffed because I refused to trade a woodstove acquired from the estate auction for one of his, the brother claimed that too many of his friends thought the epitaph disrespectful, and he pried it loose and laid it, epitaph down, into a batch of fresh cement.

This turn of events did not exactly humor me. As I pondered what to do with the rest of the log which Adolph's likeness now topped, I began to

Butternut, 30" tall, 1984
Collection of Bill & Mickey Berg
#163

wonder how he might have responded. Then it happened. While at a political fundraiser off in the countryside the candidate's son came rushing out of the kitchen door and, without the slightest hesitation or hint of modesty, exercised his prerogative right there on the back stoop. I knew right there what Adolph would have told his brother, and I finished the carving in an appropriate manner. (The brother, when he found out, was livid; but has since gotten over it...I think.)

Swedish Defiance was a bit rough in many ways, and in 1984 I decided to return to this theme. The motivation was not the social commentary that this one would contain, but rather the belief that entering competitions that year wouldn't be much fun if I didn't have at least one piece that would offend someone.

So here it is, a rendering of the classic male chauvinist pig, with an old stogie in his mouth, an NRA decal on his cap, the Schlitz Colt 45 belt buckle on his belt (as a contrast to the 22 caliber — or smaller — equipment below his belt), and a button on his chest that states "It's a man's world, honey". The subtitle for this piece is "Gawrsh, are these your petunias, Ma'am?"

This is the type of piece that doesn't appeal to everyone. Many people admired it but then shied away from its purchase — not knowing where they would display it or who it might offend if they owned it. Eventually it went to a Minneapolis police officer and his wife who dearly love it.

The Secret Is Stealth ————————

Like every other indigenous product of the "boonies", I grew up in a milieu of great white hunters and learned to revere their myths, even though I never quite understood them. Any activity which begets such zealotry is surely in need of some satire — hence this piece and its companion, "Keepin' an Eye Peeled".

This piece shows the stealthy predator intent on his mission, his trusty "blow 'em away" blunderbuss at the ready, but about to step on a branch and startle everything within earshot, including the birds perched on his hat and on the butt of his gun.

Butternut, 14" tall, 1986
Collection of Dr. Jon Bosland
#194

Keepin' an Eye Peeled

Again we visit our ever-alert great white hunter as he sits watching and waiting for his quarry to come into sight. In the meantime, he has one duck rummaging through his lunchbox while a partner in crime finishes off the would-be ambusher's can of beer. Not to worry. His stalwart companion is keeping watch.

It will rather surprise me if some don't jump to the conclusion that I am an anti-hunting activist. While I admittedly fail to comprehend the point of killing other animals if you're not going to eat them, I do believe that hunters have made themselves a necessary component of the ecosystem. It does, however, bother me greatly that so many of them are such sanctimonious social Neanderthals. I will support many of their wildlife programs, but I will also show them the irreverence they need and deserve.

Basswood, 11" tall, 1987
Private Collection
#207

Givin' Thought to Pitchin' Woo ——————

The complete and correct title of the male figure is "Givin' Thought to Pitchin' Woo — LeRoy Attends the Wahoo (Nebraska) Farmer's Grain Association's Annual Harvest Dance". His companion piece is simply titled "Wanton Wilma of Wahoo".

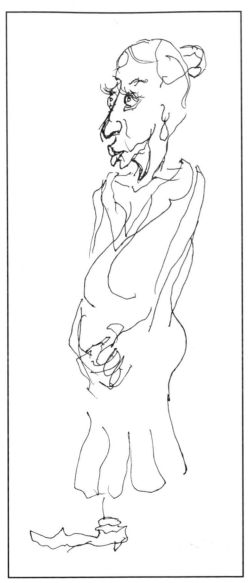

Early sketch of Wanton Wilma.

I first enjoyed the bliss of a Nebraska sojourn around 1976 when going to Walthill, Neb. to help Ron Carter mow his yard, which at the time was higher than it was wide or deep. Somehow I neglected to return until a trip to Wichita in '87. While passing through Omaha the name Wahoo just popped out from the map. I wanted to go there in the worst way. I could just imagine the yahoos from Wahoo lying about all over the place, each of them just crying out to be rendered in wood.

Detours made a visit both inconvenient and impractical, however, and I was compelled to call upon my fantasies for an appropriate Wahoo Yahoo. Certainly within this bucolic little burb there would be a Farmer's Grain Association, and amongst their harvest rituals there certainly would be an autumn dance as a prelude to the sacrificing of virgins. A portly prince of prime masculinity came to mind. The handle of "LeRoy" would certainly suit his environs well. He would be biding his time, contemplating his strategy and moves as he sought to seduce the woman of his dreams — a sweet little granny type. To make it more interesting a wanton hussy would simultaneously be lusting after LeRoy, with intentions far less honorable, and certainly less naive, than those of LeRoy.

LeRoy's finest attribute is his moonstruck expression, nicely complemented by the turn of his head, the twiddling thumbs, and the tapping toe. He is quite the contrast to Wilma, with her coquettish stance and scheming predatory stare. Her Mickey Mouse necklace says exactly what she thinks of the game.

Butternut, 13-1/5" tall, 1988
Private Collection
#217 (Leroy) & #221 (Wilma)

These pieces
are pictured
in color on
page 92.

*Study for Mabel, the planned third figure
in the Wahoo set.*

Heads and Busts

The Eyes Have It — is that how the saying goes? There's not a lot of room for innovation in sculpting portrait busts; yet there is perhaps no other area in which competence is so crucial to success for the artist who would do representational human figures. If you do not have a good face on your sculpture you have nothing. Even in a nudist colony it is the eyes and face that are first examined in an encounter (unless, of course, you are a novice naturalist). The same, with rare exceptions, holds true in sculpture.

My faces are not yet to the point of satisfying me. Development seems to be a series of plateaus. Attainment of one is followed by dissatisfaction with particular points, new areas of concentration, and a new plateau. And then the cycle is repeated.

Heaton Vorst

About the time Warren Beatty released his movie *Reds* the Sunday paper ran a large article featuring present-day photos of the folks who were young radicals at the time of the Russian revolution and which were, in fact, characters portrayed in the movie. Heaton stood out, not only for his looks but also for his name. The latter reminded me of the old Norwegian who was asked how he liked the lutefisk and answered that he'd "heaten vorse".

Butternut, 10" tall, 1982
Collection of Pearl Vruwink
#147

Mountain Man ————————————

This is the classic double-skewed expression — always one of my favorites. The line of the mouth converges with the line of the eyes. The tension on one side of the face contrasts with the placid expression on the other. The consequence is an esthetic and intriguing unit.

The face on this piece was, of course, based on the model in my mirror. The sub-title for this piece is "Hard Chew, Tough Choice".

Butternut, 15" tall, 1984
Collection of Larry Yudis (The Woodcraft Shop)
#170

Wolf Robe

This piece was inspired by a photo of Wolf Robe which adorned the cover of a friend's anthropology textbook. It was a remarkable face, with massive cheekbones and a small cranium. The disparity was so great that I assumed that much of it was due to camera distortion from a low-angle close-up with a wide-angle lens. The carving was rendered with corrective modification. Since that time the viewing of two other photos of Wolf Robe has led me to believe that the first photo, however incredible, was fairly accurate.

This bust again reflects my interest in those individuals who are caught between two different cultures, perhaps because I find myself caught between culture and non-culture. With Wolf Robe we have a man who made his mark as an Indian brave, and then chose to attire himself, in part, with the trappings of the enemy. Such choices were in some measure due to Indian beliefs in "medicine" — the belief that the spirit of an animal or enemy could be captured and used to one's own advantage by simply wearing some bit of their hide, plumage, or adornment. But it was also a reflection of the Indian's assimilation into the white man's society.

Butternut, 22" tall, 1984
Private Collection
#169

The likeness and name of General Kearney on the kerchief medallion was a bit of artistic license — a touch to underscore the ironies of the portrait. The two feathers coming off to the right at the back of his head were not broken. This is simply where the log ran out, and I had decided to confine the piece to the original block of wood. The effect is actually in keeping with the authenticity of the portrait, as eagle feathers were often notched or cut off in a variety of ways to denote the particular coup or achievement for which they stood.

Flathead Chieftain After Curtis

To my knowledge there is but one portrait by Edward Sherif Curtis in which he failed to identify the subject. That photo — the model for this piece — was simply entitled "Flathead Chieftain". The subject was entirely in traditional costume, with a hide shirt and eagle-bone war whistle. The distinguishing aspect of the subject was that he wore four, rather than two, braids.

A walnut log that had been set aside seemed particularly appropriate to the endeavor. Logs are often preferable to laminated blocks because there are no disruptions in the grain pattern and because the rings naturally accentuate the forehead, eyes, and cheeks. Walnut, however, is much more difficult to cure in a log form than is butternut, with its greater density and propensity towards checking. This particular log had the advantage of having rotted away in one quarter. This greatly reduced the tension and increased the stability of the remainder of the wood throughout the drying process.

Black Walnut, 18" tall, 1984
Collection of Chuck DeCathelineau
#158

Sculptor in Wood

Martin

Selections in Color ————————————

The Hired Men

"Gust" — *With Thoughts of Mabel*

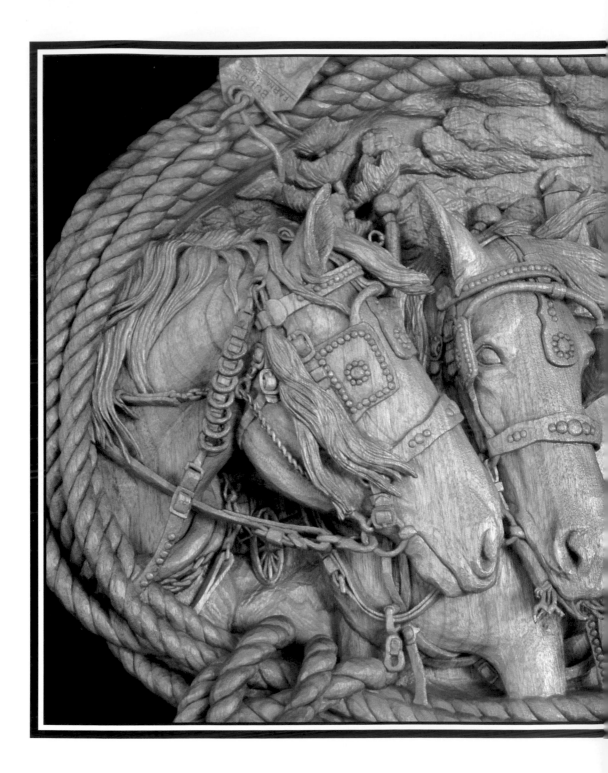

Day's End

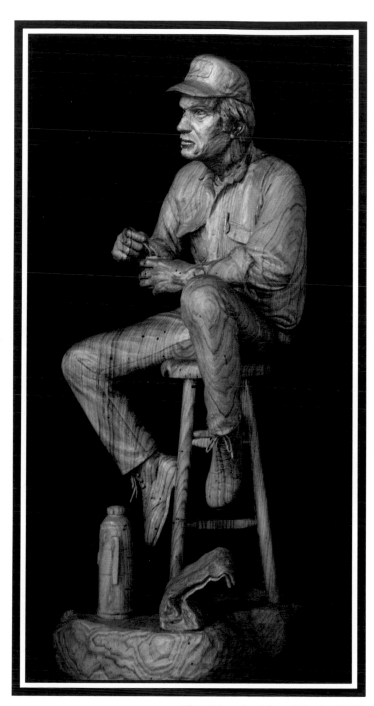

The Story's About Joe's Wife

Selections in Color

Hunts Crying Bear

Morning After Breakfast Companion

Givin' Thought to Pitchin' Woo

Aging Middle–Level Bureaucrat

Artists, by virtue of the lack of self-sufficiency in their early years, acquire tremendous loads of indebtedness to the many friends and relatives (and an occasional stranger) for their assistance along the way. The accumulated debt is more than can ever be repaid. The artist who remembers that kindness tries to repay it by helping others in need — persons who likewise stand unlikely of ever being able to repay the favor. That is not to say, however, that I have simply written off those many past instances of largess . . . .

Among those who did me a number of kind turns was Lee Hanley, Doris' brother-in-law. Lee photographed a lot of my early works, gratis, and did his damndest to promote me through the Swayed Pines Fiddle Festival. The Festival, of which Lee was a prime instigator, is held each April at St. John's University near St. Cloud, Minn., and is one of the top blue-grass events in America. That wouldn't have been much, in my case, as I couldn't fiddle a whit if you paid me a million dollars. But as providence would have it, Lee had the foresight to include an Arts Fair as part of the Festival, and made it worth my while to be part of the Art Fair for several years beginning back in 1978.

In 1984 I thought to surprise Lee by working on a likeness of him at the Festival, and so I solicited some photographs of him from his wife. Turned out that she just handed the request over to him, which took a lot of the fun out of it. The progress over the course of the one-day Fair wasn't much anyway. Some 10 months later I took some of my own photo studies, worked on it again during the 1985 Festival, and finished it shortly thereafter.

The piece shows a fair amount of sensitivity and appreciation of detail. Lee was flattered — flattered too much, in fact. So just to keep him humble I entitled it "Sympathetic Portrait of an Aging Middle-Level Bureaucrat".

Butternut, 14"tall, 1985
Collection of Lee Hanley
#175

Study of a Blind Man

In the early '80s I received permission from a local nursing home to photograph those patients whose visages I found of interest, providing that the subjects or their guardians consented. Those I fancied most were uncooperative, to say the least, and I was on the verge of retreating in despair when I noticed Oral Wilson and his visiting wife. Oral was quiet, intelligent, and cooperative. I got a number of good shots of him clasping his wife's hand which she had placed over his shoulder.

It was at least two years later (if not four) that this portrait was finally executed. It was finished, ironically, just days before he died. The bust was already sold, which made me feel a bit less awkward bringing it to the viewing at the funeral home. (Imagine, if you will, the strategy of working up busts of the terminally ill. Then rushing the finished product, without advance notice to the assembled mourning family and telling them that they have just two days in which to purchase it for $1,200 — otherwise you will glue warts on the nose and sell it for half-price at the local gallery.) My hesitation was unwarranted, however, for the wife had been wondering if anything had come from the photo session. Each family member seemed to find it a consolation that this likeness of Oral would remain.

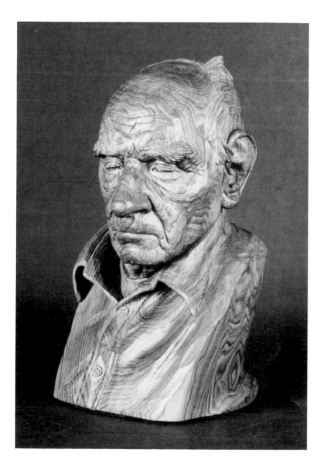

Carving a blind person presents some special challenges. The eyes tend to be closed or half-closed, and the position of the head is often much different from a sighted person. I seldom include much detail in the eyelashes, but on this piece I deemed it was necessary. The piece is executed well enough so that it should be obvious that the subject is blind. Experience however leaves me choosing to insult, with the title, the collective intelligence of the viewers.

Butternut, 13" tall, 1986
Collection of June Peick
#200

Emil Mulls a Bid —————————————

Emil started with a sketch on a placemat at a local coffee shop, which was later supplemented by my imagination. As the piece took shape it began to remind me of a certain Elmo, the brother of the fellow who had already expressed an interest in a bust in this price range. It was a safe bet that he wouldn't want to risk any offense to his brother, but also that he'd find it amusing were it to remind him of his brother, so I decided that "Emil" was a logical title. As both brothers were electrical contractors and as I already had a pencil behind his ear the title was almost a foregone conclusion.

— ✳ —

My insurance agent sometimes has fits with these titles. The additions to the policy coverage are generally given over the phone. Whether it is my lack of diction or his hearing loss, or some combination thereof, is uncertain, but the results are generally more imaginative than the original title. This one was originally insured as Emil Mauls A Bear; then Elmo Mauls a Beer. That didn't make much sense, even to him, and after a repeat it became "mauls a bed", which, after all, made some sense. It took an office visit to convince him that the verb was "mulls" — which again confused the heck out of him. "Mulls a bed?!!" he exclaimed in disbelief, incredulous that I would have such an incomprehensible title. . . . then we finally got it right.

Butternut, 11" tall, 1985
Collection of Frank and Shirley Chapin
#177

Not-So-Stiff Upper Lip

This is a bit of a repeat. The first was called "The Stiff Upper Lip" and was carved for my good friend Bob Peick when he was facing surgery for cancer. He liked it immensely, though it never did a hell of a lot for him as a good luck charm.

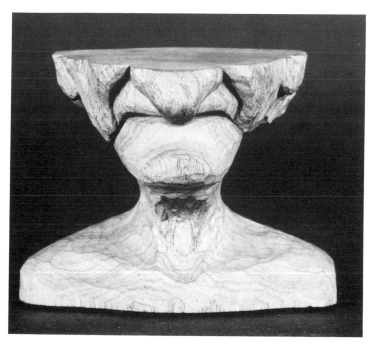

Butternut, 3-1/2" high
1987

Doris hit the big "4–0" shortly thereafter, an occasion which seemed to make her equally deserving. Being merely 38 myself at the time, and understanding that one's teeth might well fall out immediately upon crossing that threshold, I naturally made hers a "not-so-stiff" upper lip. Bob's must not have impressed her, cause the separately presented pieces totally mystified her.

Maybe some day she'll look back fondly at it. For now, it's safe to say that other gifts have thrilled her more.

Neil's Feeds

Neil Cox is somewhere between "up and coming" and "being there" as an outstanding woodcarver. We first met at the Durham Wood Show in Ontario in August of 1986. He'd left word that if I showed up he would like to meet me. Naturally suspicious of anyone who would want to meet me, I assumed the identity of fellow carver John Sharp, my travelling companion, and coerced John into assuming mine. The next few hours, as I enjoyed dinner and they tried to, I exhibited my worst behaviors, while John was his usual proper and genteel self. My performance left Neil thinking that this Sharp fellow I was pretending to be was the most crude and infantile fellow he had ever met. The next day at the Wood Show we informed others of our switch, and asked them to keep the secret. It was well into our next encounter, some three weeks later, that Neil figured out the truth.

Fortunately, Neil is the only fellow I know who is positively more good-hearted than John Sharp, and enjoyed the deception rather than holding it against me. A couple years later we hired him to do some pieces for our newly-remodeled home. He did them so reasonably that I felt obligated to do one for him.

The carving for Neil was based on a photo of an old Norwegian bachelor farmer whom I had known for many years. His name was Alfred Halvorson, and the picture was among the earliest photographs I had ever taken. The scene had been a farm auction near the Stearns County line on a November day, with a temperature of something around 10 below zero. Old Alfred was just there for something to do, impervious to the cold, and not in the least bothered if I took his photograph.

The carving was very much free-handed, and was intended to simply be an interesting farm face rather than a portrait of Alfred. All the same, I was very much flattered when my cousin, who had grown up as Alfred's neighbor, saw a brief shot of the piece during some television coverage of my 1989 Duluth exhibit and immediately recognized the subject.

When Neil finally took possession of the bust he professed to be very pleased with it; particularly with the "Neil's Feeds" I had engraved on the hat to personalize it. Word from his home in Ingersoll, Ontario, however, has it that he hollowed out the back, enlarged the nostrils, and the moment he got home, nailed it to a tree, to serve as a wren house.

Guess that's his business. He's still a welcome guest here anytime. Should you ever get the opportunity to host him, seize it. He'll entertain you mightily, repair your broken electronics, and even make up a best-you-ever-tasted batch of that most sinful Wisconsin dessert, the "Chocolate Eau Claire." And he's probably the only carver you'll ever meet who's willing to take half his pay in ice cream.

Butternut,
10" tall excluding base, 1988
Collection of Neil Cox
#225

Marie's Uncle

This is a bust which was made for my mother-in-law, Marie Binger, in return for all the many favors which she has bestowed on us over the years. It reminded her of her uncle — hence the title. It is a basswood relief based on another photo taken at the same November auction which provided the photos of Alfred used on the Neil's Feeds bust. It was a very cold day, and the farmer's moustache was completely coated with his frozen breath.

This is one of the few carvings for which it was decided to omit the irises and pupils — in this case to impart a bit of that blank and distant frozen look. This piece also reflects a further simplification of form; a quasi-realistic style that started with "Emil Mulls a Bid". This style is appealing, and it remains to be seen if it merits a life-size rendition at some point.

Basswood, 7" tall, 1988
Collection of Marie Binger
#229

The preliminary sketch
for "Marie's Uncle."

Iowa Hogeyes

The story behind this mask is that of old Ole, a Norwegian bachelor farmer from that bunch of Norskies that settled into the wooded ravines of Southwestern Minnesota. The story is that he had a nephew to the south who invited him to come down for the University of Iowa homecoming game. Wanting to show his ardent support for the hometown team, Ole decided to make up his own booster's cap and come prepared. He'd thought he had heard his nephew call them the Hawkeyes, but he knew that couldn't be right, being that Iowa is the pig state, so he fixed up a cap to read "Iowa Hogeyes", and resolved to get his hearing checked just as soon as he returned.

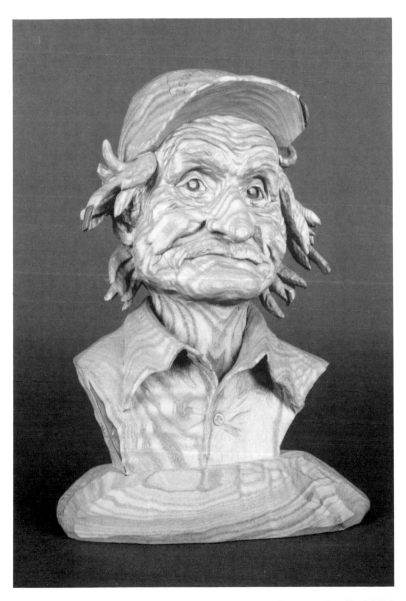

Catalpa, 11" tall, 1988
Collection of Joanne Coussens Rumpza
 # 211

Small Faces and Busts

Noelle owns and operates the Our Frame Shop and Gallery, the establishment which represents me locally. I'm not the easiest guy to work with, and she never knows when she'll be getting something new or how long it will be staying before it leaves for some competition or exhibition. Yet she bends over backwards for me, and she isn't a bit shy when it comes to advertising. My only complaint is that another name for the place would certainly sound a lot more glamorous, even if most of her business is framing prints for the fellows who want the depictions of ducks flying left and ducks flying right and ducks coming in and ducks heading out. So when she asked me if I could make up a few moderate-priced items for a November open house, I grudgingly (based on past performance of such items) agreed. Much to my surprise, they sold like hot cakes. In the two years since I've been cranking out between one and two dozen of the little buggers, and it seems to keep everybody happy.

They're somewhat of a pleasure to carve after you've been racking your brains on a complicated piece for a month or better, or when the interruptions become so frequent that you just can't concentrate — or remember the mental notes you made to yourself just a quarter-hour earlier. And being not so serious, these small carvings allow you to loosen up some, and to experiment a bit.

After you've done about five or six straight the pleasure diminishes dramatically, however, which gives me pause concerning remarks I have made about spending eternity with my chisels. In fact, having slept on those bold assertions for a night I suspect that, given my druthers, I'd opt to leave my chisels behind and make a beeline for the concupiscent attractions of a Hindu hereafter.

Carving is an unmitigated pleasure as long as it's totally mindless, and the chisel is sharp, and the wood is cooperative — but I fear that those are rather fleeting circumstances when they occur, and that they rarely happen in the first place. There have been far too many hours of back-wrenching bending over interminable reliefs, of standing on my head trying to access the inaccessible on a statue, and of boring myself to death trying to correct the uncorrectable — fudging and compromising close to half the carving just to give a hasty commitment the appearance of amazing decisiveness and rectitude.

Who knows? Maybe in eternity I'll be of a mind to take up fishing. . ...Naw, who wants to just sit around when they could be doing something?

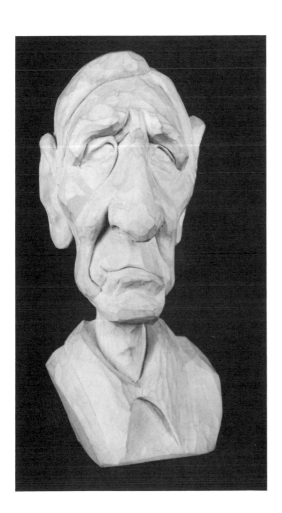

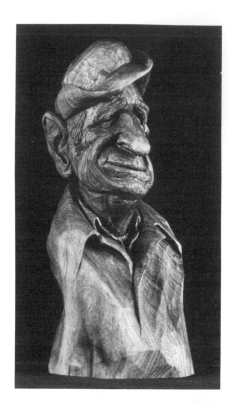

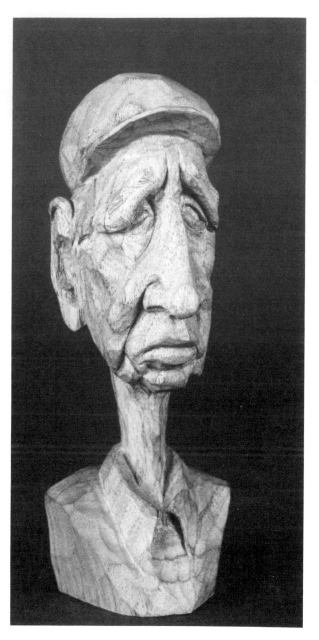

Grandpa's Smile

This bust in wormy butternut comes from a photo of the model whose face was used for "Martin". My wife likes him, saying he reminds her of her uncle Swen. I've never had the courage to ask whether it was the expression or the thick skull that served as the reminder.

Seriously, it was a case in which I undercut the ears too soon, leaving myself with the choice of giving him either an excessively broad skull or a pair of elephant ears. The first option was selected. Fortunately, with such a sweet smile he isn't much diminished by having a fat head.

Butternut, 10" tall, 1986
Collection of Doris Cogelow
#197

Two Trees ————————————

Eastern aromatic red cedar has always appealed to me. It's a dramatic wood, with very pronounced colors. And if you're going to do an Indian, why not do it in a red wood? Cedar is, unfortunately, not a good carving wood, as it splits easily and tends to be very knotty.

This piece is based on an Indian named Two Trees whom Neil Cox brought to my attention. The head-dress is simply a cloth wrapped around his head, with some feathers stuck between his head and the cloth.

Cedar, 18" tall, 1989
Private Collection
#220

Relief Carvings

It was with reliefs that I first made my mark. The early ones were timid affairs — most of them portraits (similar, but less elaborate, than "Mother and Child"), cautiously etched out in bas-relief. Limited successes, however, were sufficient to increase both confidence and ambition.

The process, as with sculpting in the round, is fortunately a logical one, demanding no special erudition or knowledge of esoterica. Its requirements are simply that you think, see, and try. That, in combination with the perception that there was a dearth of exemplary relief carving on the continent, led to a conscious decision, following the completion of the piece called "Brothers Posing", to prove that I could at least, in part, fill that void.

Relief carving, particularly towards the low end of the scale, is in essence little more than line enhancement. Line outweighs mass in the eye's perception of these works, and it is the propriety and esthetics of the line structure which are of the utmost importance. Once a worthy subject or motif has been selected the impression of depth can be created through a variety of devices: converging lines, overlapping forms, foreshortening, and diminution of size with distance. Proper execution then accentuates that feeling of depth with exploitation of actual carving depth and undercutting. Some designs require more subtlety and sophistication in execution than do others; e.g. the smaller and more isolated the foreground elements are the easier it becomes to carve them almost in the round.

The general rule-of-thumb is that your foreground elements warrant 75-90% of the actual depth for their execution. A great number of classical high reliefs are, in fact, little more than in-the-round subjects defined by a bas-relief backdrop. Proper sophistication requires that the use and reuse of depth and background elements should be given as much actual thickness as they can congruously receive — but in most scenarios they can suffice with the most minimum of enhancements.

In high relief carving there is no absolute right or wrong approach, but only things that could have been done better or worse. That is simultaneously one's greatest reassurance and most nagging curse; done well, it is hard to prove that the sculptor erred, but it is equally hard to prove he/she couldn't have done better.

Brothers Posing

In 1981, at an auction north of town, a local family practitioner asked my opinion of a particular piece of furniture. In subsequent conversations it came out that he had heard of me, and that he was interested in purchasing a carving — maybe. A good while later we met again and he said he would like a carving for the waiting room of his new office, then under construction. Three options were put together and he rejected all three, suggesting that he would instead prefer a farm scene with animals and children. I then produced a photo of my father and his brother when they were kids, standing next to a wagon in a pose designed to look cute, and told him that I could do something with it. The doctor didn't seem entirely convinced, but told me to go ahead with it anyway.

The picture selected as a focal point for the carving was a good one — a couple of decidedly posed urchins with their old wooden coaster wagon, sporting smiles that hinted that they were both devils and angels. My father was wriggling his toes, giving indications of being a little restive.

To give the carving added definition various elements from their childhood were added to the design. Their home appears in the background as it looked then. The old barn, the wheelbarrow, and one of the cars came from their old photo albums. Horses were not much of a part of my Father's life until his late adolescence, and then they were a mania — so I included them. Last, but not least, the three Norway Spruce trees were planted by their guardian, my great aunt Agnes when she was, herself, a child. (Two of them still survive today along the property line. When those lots were sold she made the new owners promise never to cut them down as long as she lived. She made such an impression that one of the buyers passed it along as a condition of a subsequent sale. One of the neighbors is still waiting for her to die,

Mahogany, 22"h x 38"w x 2-1/2"thick, 1982
Collection of Dr. Lyle Munneke

even though she's been gone for the past twenty years.)

The new design was resubmitted. The Doctor wasn't thrilled but he allowed as, with the inclusion of some barnyard poultry, the carving could commence. The completed piece met with a much warmer response. After some reassuring compliments from his clientele he was ready for another piece.

— ✳ —

The piece now hangs in the good doctor's waiting room. Judging by the continuing strong favorable reaction to it, most people are not bothered in the least by its technical shortfalls, of which there are several. Most disturbing is that the actual depth was neither fully or properly exploited and there is an incongruent diminution within the background.

Then again, they seem to pain only me. The blessing to having committed these sins (one might get the impression that my behind was, in its youth, rather familiar with the contours of a church pew) is that they troubled me sufficiently that I resolved not to commit them ever again.

To admit its imperfections is not to say that I dislike the piece — quite the contrary. Brothers Posing has both technical merits and a basic esthetic and nostalgic appeal. It was also an important piece from a developmental standpoint. While another's photograph remained the core of the piece, the majority of this fairly complicated design was original and required substantial manipulation and fabrication of detail, and portions of the original photo were also modified (the direction of their wagon's front wheels and handle was changed and a shirt and pail were placed inside it). Additionally it was the first piece to manifest an obsession with undercutting — carving around and behind the various elements to the greatest possible extent. Finally, it was my first piece to incorporate a laminated foreground element which spilled out of and over the frame for purposes of increasing the depth exploitation options within the main slab.

Photo of my father and his brother.

The Hired Men

It wasn't long after I delivered "Brothers Posing" to the doctor that he indicated he had developed a belated interest in one of the three designs he had rejected earlier — one with two old men in front of a pair of open french doors leading to a garden court. I had planned to do it anyway, but just couldn't find the subjects I needed. This stalemate continued until the Christmas of 1982 when my sister, Linda, and her husband, Ron, gave me a Time-Life book on photography as a gift.

Bless their souls. There on opposite pages were two Paul Strand photos of a French sailor and a French vineyard worker. They were exactly what I had wanted. The photos were murky, but they held or hinted at all the requisite detail, right down to a cigarette butt clasped between the thumb and index finger of the vintner's left hand.

But the people in these photos were too good for the background I had in mind. So I decided that, as they were French, I would make them French-Canadian farm laborers and use, as a backdrop, the inside of an old, heavy-timbered Ontario barn. So books on old wooden barns were consulted. An imaginary barn interior was drawn up and bits of miscellaneous rope and harness and some barn swallow nests were added.

It was carved from a 2-1/4" thick slab, with another 2-1/4" piece laminated to the front for the face, hat, and lapels of the lower figure. It's probably the most correct relief carving that I've done. The figures are powerful, but in a quiet way. The background is defining and busy, but not inordinately so. The use of converging lines and diminishing beam sizes is an easy but effective way to give the impression of depth. The actual depth used for each element is in accordance with it's significance in the design.

The good doctor didn't know it was coming until shortly before it arrived. He was quite impressed and asked the price. I hesitated, and he told me to be fair to myself. After further hemming and hawing, I gave him a figure to which he readily agreed. It was quite an occasion to have someone tell me to be fair to myself. Others had treated me with respect, but the prevailing attitude seemed to be that artists are supposed to be poor and miserable. To have someone encourage me to be fair to myself was a prospect I had never expected. Needless to say, it left me with a special regard for the man.

This piece was named Best-of-Show at the 1983 International Woodcarving Exposition in Toronto. What a delight. Got me to fantasizing that maybe, just maybe, I was finally on my way....

This piece is
pictured in
color on
page 86.

Mahogany, 26"h x 17w x 4-1/2"thick, 1983
Collection of Dr. Lyle Munneke
#154

The Swing is Gone

The "Swing is Gone" is the story of an old extended barn and the generations whose lives were so closely entwined with it. Built by the first generation (shown at the top in the left column) and added upon by both of the succeeding generations, and perhaps by the Grandpa himself, it now stands unused and falling into disrepair. The boy's father (absent from the carving) left the farm to make his living elsewhere, breaking the continuity of generations which the barn depended upon to keep it from decay. The boy is melancholic, not because his metaphoric "swing" is gone, but because he has returned to find that, even at his tender age, the realities do not match the memories. He realizes that time is change — inexorable change — and he knows that before long the aging Grandpa and the aging barn, both dear to him, will both be gone.

The barn was photographed in late 1983 just outside Palatine Bridge, New York. There were many dates burned into some of the massive beams of the interior, mostly from the late 1700's. But the date 1832 (also found inside) was used to provide a more reasonable span of time for the story of six generations.

The old man is based on two photos of my old friend Adolph Highstrom, a "brush yankee" Swede bachelor who spent his prime years tending cows in the wooded gravel hills near Games and Skull Lakes in northern Kandiyohi County. Prior to his death in May, 1981 Adolph spent many years helping me at the sawmill, teaching me how to identify trees, explaining the art of postponing puberty in cows with epsom salts, and warning of the evils of chewing tobacco.

The boy was photographed at an art fair in downtown Minneapolis in July of 1977. Of the ancestors, the first, second, and fourth were based on photos from the book *Wisconsin Death Trip*. The third was my Great-grandfather John Nelson from Hills, Minnesota. The last two were a nameless Great-uncle and Great-aunt from the Morris area. The models were selected simply on the basis of character and suitability of hairstyles and attire.

Old Man Kench (and the Ladies)

In the summer of 1984 I started thinking about a relief carving with antique automobiles. The effort to compose a design with my camera resulted in the creation of a half dozen carvings, none of which has the slightest thing to do with cars. Among those have been "Old Man Kench", "Martin", and "Married Her in '33".

The pursuit of the idea led me, in September, 1984, to Pioneer Days in Avon, a town about 40 miles northeast of Willmar. It was there that I encountered a fellow named Ralph Budde parading about with his team of Belgians pulling an antique manure spreader. I was always nuts about heavy horses so I hopped aboard and asked him for some photo studies while he unhitched the girls for the ride home.

Of the studies taken, two were initially selected as prospects for relief carvings. The face and clothes were changed, substituting something a bit more agrarian for Ralph's cowboy hat and western denim jacket. A composite background was then added based on the farm owned by Valerie Kench, just outside Gananoque, Ontario.

Valerie Kench is a story all by herself. In August, 1983, I stopped by her place to ask directions and recommendations to motels in the area. She was out front at the time, saying goodnight to a visiting son and his wife, and coldly but politely opined that all the motels would be full with firemen attending a national convention. Some checking quickly proved her to be correct. I returned and asked to park behind her barn and sleep in the back of my truck.

She wasn't quite sure what to make of my audacity, but she consented. The following morning she fixed me breakfast and gave a tour of the barns. I stopped to see her again each of the next two summers, and wish it were possible to stop there each and every summer. Valerie is wonderfully well-informed and

Butternut, 29" wide x 23" high x 3-1/4" thick, 1985
Collection of M/M Tom Torgerson
#171

thoughtful about life and the world around her. She's also one of the most cynical, if not outright morbid, people I have ever known. But she intersperses her melancholy and despair with enough humor that the visitor has a fine time. The fact that she spends some of her spare time teaching convicts to read has me thinking that she is, in truth, a closet optimist.

I stole her name for the title, as is obvious. Ralph Budde's name is pronounced "buddy", and that conjured up images of sailors on shore leave—so I borrowed Kench for its pleasing sound.

This was the first piece where I became absolutely serious about using all the available depth. With this and other framed pieces that followed there is at least one area where it is possible to see light coming through the back when the piece is held up to a light source.

"Old Man Kench" was well received at the shows, taking Best-of-Show at Toronto in 1985. At the Davenport show it took the Wakefield Award for "uncommon and exceptional interpretation and execution of subject matter", plus the first-ever People's Choice Award presented there.

Death Mask of a Polish Laborer ——

Anyone with a local reputation in this business gets a number of requests each year from folks who'd like to sell or simply get rid of a black walnut yard tree. The usual excuse is that they're "too messy". If the same criterion and solutions were applied to humanity by the Deities our species would be quickly obliterated. I generally use that reasoning and an appeal to the owner's environmental responsibility to gain the tree another lease on life.

In the case of one tree which was shading an intended garden spot, I was a bit late. The tree was down by the time I got there. To make the crime worse, the fellow who had taken it down wasn't about to get on his knees, and had made the felling cuts about three feet above the ground. As a final insult he did this so ineptly that the stump was split. Always one to salvage as much as possible, I split out a hunk about 5" thick and a foot wide and set it aside with a mask in mind.

Masks have always appealed to me. After a few admiring looks at my favorite model in the mirror it was decided that we would try for a carving with possessed laughter. (Actually the fellow in the mirror is not my favorite model, but he is the most convenient — and he usually understands what it is that I am attempting.)

The pattern was drawn directly on the wood and was executed with frequent glances into the reflective glass. As it neared completion it reminded me of my good Polish friend who involved me in that church door project, and of his way of laughing — hence the full title "Death Mask of a Polish Laborer Who Last October Succumbed to a Wisconsin Happy Hour".

Black Walnut, 18"h, 1986
Collection of Drs. Nila &
Darko Florschutz
#196

Martin

Martin is one of my favorite pieces; a combination of detailed simplicity, charming demeanor, and affection. It is a memorial to my old "back forty" Swede bachelor and chief sawmill assistant, Adolph.

Adolph ran his stories like a record playing over and over again. He had a couple of dozen stories which made up 90 % of his conversation for the last decade of his life. Among them was the story about when he almost got married. It seemed that he was working on a threshing crew at a local farm where the daughter had a particular fondness for him. Whenever mealtime or bad weather caused a break in the work the two would spend some time in innocent and interminable coquetry. But Adolph had a basic bashfulness and fear of women which prevented him from seriously pursuing the fairer sex. The girl in this instance realized that if she were to wait until Adolph made the first move she'd be fairly well fossilized before any manner of proposal would issue from Adolph's lips. So when the threshing crew finished in the early afternoon of the last day she suggested to Adolph that they go to town and get married. Adolph nearly spit out his teeth! He wasn't entirely certain of her sincerity, but he was absolutely sure there was some degree of earnestness in her suggestion.

Unfortunately there was another fellow on the threshing crew (whom Adolph disliked) who had the "hots" for this particular woman. He was within easy earshot of the couple when the girl made the suggestion. He too almost spit out his teeth, but recovered soon enough to state that if Adolph and the girl were going to town to wed then he was going to go with them.

"Well," said Adolph, "if he's going to town then I ain't." And that was that . . . sort of. She never repeated the offer, at least not to Adolph. And Adolph could never quite get her memory — or a certain fantasy — out of his mind. Fifty-five years later he was still telling the story on a monthly basis with a tangible air of regret to his tale. For as long as he lived that lady remained the fair young maiden of his youth. It seemed everytime he turned back the mental pages to consort with her he was only 25 years old himself.

So here we have Martin — a diminutive, sweet old guy, holding onto the ancient photograph of his childhood sweetheart, still loving her now for the dream she was then. Hence, the full and proper title, "Loved Her Then, Still Loves Her Now...or, Still Loves Now What She Was Then."

The hat Martin wears is based on an old hat in Adolph's collection of junk, but that's the only physical bearing he has on the piece. The fellow whose face was used as a model was an old-timer from Sauk Centre. I met the spindly old guy and his substantial friend at the

Albany Pioneer Days, and took a number of photos of the pair in and around some old automobiles.

Howard Gray was the model for Martin's body. A friend told me about Howard, and brought him over to be photographed. I took about a hundred photos of Howard and another old sport, an old baseballer named Virgil Gabbert. None of the photos quite did the job, and they refused to return for another session. But Howard allowed me to go over to his place on short notice and shoot him for other studies, one of which eventually became Martin's body. I made Howard remove his tie, messed up his collar, and put a ragged old denim jacket on him. There was no need to install the bib overalls. Howard always wore bib overalls and a tie.

This piece is pictured in color on page 85.

Butternut, 48"h x 17"w x 3"thick, 1986
Collection of Dr. Jon Bosland
#192

Day's End

I thought "Day's End" would be a great name for a motel, but never had much inspiration to carve one. This work is, of course, based on another photo study singled out from the Budde shots. And again, the background is a composite from the Kench farm.

One of the elements that intrigued me with both of these carvings (Day's End and Old Man Kench) was the blinders on the horses' bridles. The idea of finding an eye behind a flap of leather seems to have an appeal all of its own. Maybe it's only because I'm a visual artist — but I think it's probably more general than that.

I always have liked oval frames, and suspect that they are more esthetic. Corners are a nasty distraction. But I don't know if I'll ever be dumb enough to do a rope frame again. Talk about tedium ad nauseam . . . thought I'd die.

Got my chance to acknowledge Budde with this one. On the tag I engraved "Budde Farm Supply", along with the title, the carving number, and my logo.

Design changes required the addition of some wood for the right half of the tag and insertion of another block for the fence and foliage to the right of the fellow. It was otherwise carved entirely as one piece and was executed without any breakage.

This piece is pictured in color on page 88.

Butternut, 21"h x 24"w x 3-1/4"thick, 1986
Collection of M/M William Warren
#193

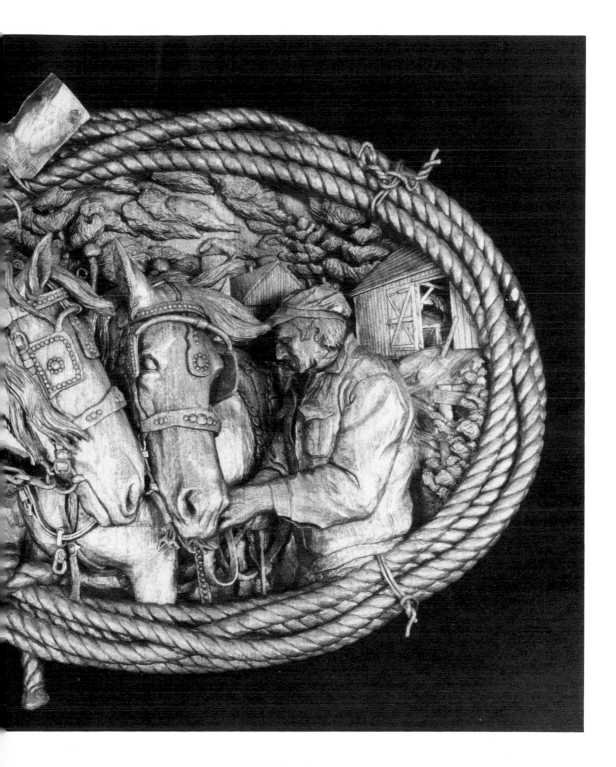

Easter Relief

My old friend, Adolph, was pretty much a loner. I suspect that many of those who sought him out in his later years fancied him vulnerable — liable for a quick demise — and suited to their pecuniary interests. Others were definitely above such conduct, such as Harvey Hanson, who entered the picture in somewhat of a guardian capacity and later served as executor of the estate. Harvey bought the farm himself a couple of years later, and early in '85 his widow came to request a memorial. His treatment of Adolph secured a positive response, and this relief was the consequence.

This was one of those pieces which involved quite a number of people in the design. Numerous gatherings of friends were subjected to the indignities of donning bedsheets and dramatically posturing themselves before my camera — all without any real success. Eventually it fell to my sister Linda and Ron, her husband, to do most of the posing. Ron was the model for John and for both of the crucified figures. The latter poses found him in his cut-offs, lashed to their daughter's play-gym. Yours truly, with numerous and significant (though not entirely satisfactory) permutations, was the model for Mary Magdalene. (Ah! This could inspire yet another Madonna video.)

The scene is very traditional, and its artistic renderings through the centuries probably number in the hundreds. It is perhaps in my original treatment of it that I take the most pride. The prime characters, in addition to Christ, are His mother, John (whom He instructed to care for her), and Mary Magdalene. The subjects are set between and slightly behind Jesus and the cross to His right (out of view).

This composition allowed me several possibilities. First, there was no compulsion to show the face of Christ, a task for which I lacked the audacity. Second, it allowed for the infusion of drama to the cross. The cross beam conforms to perspective, and thrusts out at the viewer. The vertical beam defies perspective, and enlarges as it towers above, making a statement about its significance and preeminence. The backward lean accentuates it all.

It was a difficult piece in many respects, much of it emanating from the perceived necessity of overlapping Mary, John, and Christ. The relief does contain one insertion — the scroll above Christ's head was originally forgotten.

The theme is actually tangential to the crucifixion. It is rather significant that an omnipotent Deity should command a mortal to take care of his bereaved mother, and the message ought not be taken casually by His followers.

Butternut, 24"wide x 27"high x 3-1/8"deep, 1987
Collection of Peace Lutheran Church
#199

Relief Carvings

The Folks

Most family albums are atrocities begging to be forgotten. Those of my wife's mother are, to the contrary, exemplary in their quantity of fine photos. Among them are a number of interesting shots of her grandparents — good Swedes who always stood a double-arm's length apart and leaned in opposite directions. It leaves one to suspect that immaculate conception may have been a more mundane phenomenon than first believed.

This double portrait required placing them a little closer together. The hand was added as an integrating symbol and made oversize for effect. While I ordinarily disdain glasses on carvings, they seemed quite esthetic and appropriate in this piece — and are, of course, carved from the original blocks of wood.

The grain in this piece warranted special attention. The faces were the primary concern, but I did not want a harsh grain disjuncture through her shoulder which conventional edge-joining would have left. In consequence the pieces were carved separately and then overlapped, with a complicated glove-fit joint the result.

This piece was used on the promotional posters and T-shirts made up for my '89 displays in Duluth and Chicago.

Butternut, 11" tall x 18" wide x 3" deep, 1988
Collection of Lyle & Bea Johnson
#218

Married Her in '33 —————————————————

The complete title of this piece is "Married Her in '33 . . . Should've Waited a Few Years", and it reflects my predilection for ambiguous or misleading titles. The title has nothing to do with any regrets for a bachelorhood ended too soon. It is instead a lament for hard times that might have been eased or avoided with a nuptial delay.

Howard and Hermina Gray tied the knot in 1933, and invested the little money they had in farming . . . and children — five girls, one after the other. Bang's disease decimated their dairy herd as things went from bad to worse, and the farm was lost. "Man, it was tough, I tell ya," Howard said, recalling those times. "You'd come home from a whole day of looking for work with nothing to show for it and then look at the faces of those hungry little babies and know there wasn't a thing you could do about it. Man, it was tough . . .." His eyes misted at the thought. "We really should've waited a few years. . . "

Yet, for all their trials, things worked out. First came a job manually digging trenches for new waterlines. Then a good job as a heavy-equipment operator. The girls all grew up healthy, got married, and had children of their own. Hermina stayed with him until his death in March, 1988. ...Perhaps they were right not to have waited.

This work was started on January 1, 1987, to have an interesting piece in progress for a state capitol display as part of the "Best of Minnesota" festivities held in conjunction with the Governor's inaugural. It took Best-of-Show honors in 1987 at both the International Woodcarvers' Congress at Davenport and at the Canadian International Exhibition in Toronto, making it the first piece to ever win both shows in the same year. In 1988 it was named Best-of-Show at the Woodcarver's Showcase at Silver Dollar City in Branson, Missouri.

Butternut, 32"h x 35"w x 5-1/2" thick, 1987
Collection of John & Hazel Chaney
#205

Rural Requiem

Losing a farm is a pain that takes generations to go away. While there are a few who will show their open wounds to the public, it seems that for the majority of farmers it is a defeat so embarrassing that bringing it back in conversation is almost as agonizing as the original loss. Instead it is swept under the rug of stoic reticence — but all the same continues to surface in a quiet but persistent manner.

My Great-grandfather John Nelson had about a square mile spread in the very southwest corner of Minnesota — some of the best farmland in the country. He divided it amongst his three sons before retiring. Grandpa got a mighty nice 220-acre spread of which he took particular care. He was, for the most part, a cautious man. But he borrowed money for a new barn with a 12 volt wind generator electrical system, wired the house, and added some of the other amenities while he was at it. Worse yet, he co-signed notes in the late '20s with his father, a believer in the virtues of acquiring even more land. Then the bottom fell out. Tough times for farmers started while the rest of the country was still riding high, but Nels hung on into the early '30s before losing it all. (Perhaps if he had sold half the farm early on he would've come out better, but he held on to it all until the bitter end.)

Once the farm was gone he packed up his wife and kids and moved 150 miles to the northeast, which was where Ma eventually met Pa, with yours truly among the consequences. They rented another farm, this one not so nice, and continued to work it until the mid '50s. The most palpable result of going down with the first farm was an extreme reluctance to borrow any money, unless it was absolutely unavoidable; a caution which was drilled into their children and their children's children. Thus were ruined two generations of venture capitalists.

Sculptor in Wood

Butternut, 26"high x 35"wide, 1988
Collection of Four Lakes Colorgraphics
#213

I never lived on a farm, but used to enjoy my limited work on them — baling hay, and feeding the cattle and hogs. Chickens weren't a particular joy — but they weren't so bad, either. The worst experiences seemed to be helping the ladies weed the garden or pick strawberries. Spent most of my time with cousin David, for whom these tasks were not a pleasant interlude but the drudgery of everyday. The time I spent with David and his Dad were sufficient to plant a lingering empathy and affection in me for those who till the soil, and then bring their dusty dollars to town and soil the tills. All the same I have never quite figured them out. It's a job that requires eternal optimism, yet when you listen to them they seem to all be permanently depressed pessimists.

— ✳ —

The idea for this piece actually came from the machinery portion of a draft horse auction. The auctioneer had his back to me and the men were gathered about an old single-bottom plow; and in watching them I could not help but feel that they were gathered about an altar while their high-priest conducted his ritual. I combined five or six photographs with some free-handing and additional background faces to come up with the entire scene.

It was originally started on a piece of 2-1/4 inch slab of honduras mahogany. That endeavor was abandoned when two-thirds complete for a variety of esthetic, technical, and superstitious reasons. It's resurrection in five inches of butternut involved a significant departure from my customary approach. A 2-1/2 inch base slab was joined up and partially carved before three additional sections of up to 3 inches thick were laminated to the bottom front.

A reckless error in roughing out below the arm of the second fellow on the left created numerous headaches and a major opportunity. That mistake was, in fact, the reason for delaying the final laminations for as long as possible. It also made it possible to insert a fellow behind the kitchen door in the inset and to place a crude figure of myself behind the head of the first fellow on the left. The center portion of his head (fellow on left) in the base slab was removed, and the remaining outline split loose from the back. It was then glued to the back of the piece which would eventually overlay it prior to the latter's lamination. With the obstacles removed a likeness of myself was easily added where only the most curious and observant would find it.

Rural Requiem was certainly influenced by my empathies with those who have lost their farms to foreclosure — yet I chose not to make its focus that narrow. It is simply the story of change, and it is

In-progress photo, before the left outer piece was laminated to carving. The blackened area (upper left) was drilled away to a depth of two inches, and the shaded area was then split loose and glued to the back of the piece readied for lamination — thus allowing convenient carving of the back side of the face and inclusion of a background portrait of the artist.

not known whether the precipitating circumstance was retirement, the death of the husband, or financial woes. Similarly, it is unknown whether the fellow seen entering the door in the inset is her husband, a friend, an unsympathetic creditor, or the auctioneer — and his message is likewise left to surmise. The only certainty is that her life has been changed dramatically.

The wife, incidentally, is taken from a mirror-image of a news photo of Yelena Bonner, wife of the late Andrei Sakharov.

Lollie and Burt at the Auction

While attending an auction in the spring of '86 I saw in the bundled animosity of their icy stares a portrait of this rural couple silently expressing their disdain for the intrusion of a camera-bearing city slicker into the sacrosanct confines of their venerated bucolic institution — certainly an awful lot to see in any couple's faces.

The story I imagined for them goes like this: "Her name was Lola, but her old man always called her his "little lollipop". Hence the nickname Lollie, which stuck with her. Together she and Burt raised four boys through good times and bad. These stalwart North Dakota Norwegians never went anywhere until Burt hurt his knee in 1985. He ain't worked since, so they've got plenty of time to hit all the auctions within 50 miles of home. They never seem to buy anything, except a box of junk now and again. Mostly they just stand around and watch the other folks and look friendly — unless they see you watching them."

Technically speaking this was the most tedious, if not difficult, relief carving to date. Burt is roughly 51" tall and was carved from a 3" slab. His slab overlays Lollie who was carved from a 1" slab, 39" tall. The challenge was to avoid flat, colorless renditions while refusing the temptation of harsh and exaggerated cutbacks which are contrary to my style. With Burt's face, the one area with adequate depth

(4"), the problem was exploiting the full thickness without creating too great a disparity between his face and hers. The final challenge resulted from the decision to avoid grain pattern disruption. This mandated that both figures be partially carved and that suitable stock be joined to the back of Burt's head and shoulders prior to lamination. It also required that the stock added behind his right shoulder and arm be contoured for an exact fit prior to joining the pair. Other than that, it was simple.

Butternut, 53" tall, 1989
Collection of Minnesota
Historical Society
#234

Relief Carvings

She'll Keep Him Anyway ────────────

This is a portrait of an old woman and her stroke-afflicted 94 year old husband. He is based on a real model, a newspaper photograph of an old "ranger" from northern Minnesota. She is imaginary, aside from her mouth (which also came from the newspaper photograph).

There was a strong temptation to make the full title "His brain done followed his teeth right out of his head", or "She's got more on her hat than he's got in his head, but she'll keep him anyway", but my fondness for misleading titles ends at the point of ambiguity. The intent of this work is not to be in the least disrespectful of the subjects.

Speed Isn't Everything

June of '90 found me, the illustrious President of the Affiliated Wood Carvers, Ltd., in the Quad Cities some five days in advance of the Woodcarving Congress, staying with the family of Larry Yudis — a diminutive soul with a spirit of sublime proportions. Larry was (and still is) the workhorse, almost literally, behind the Iowa competition, and we had visions of achieving an organizational coup de grace or two in advance of the event. During that time, I saw a small photograph at the top of the front page of the local newspaper. The picture happened to be of a father giving his rather ebullient son a ride upon his shoulders. The shot was immediately recognized as source material.

The photo was unfortunately left behind, compelling me to seek new models. It was decided that a grandpa sort would be best suited for the adult role and, after ruling out those who were suggested to me, the recollection dawned of noting, at a Lions' pancake breakfast some years earlier, the particularly esthetic visage of my cousin "Kelly." He was agreeable, and through my resourceful sister we found a young coquette for the child and, as a backup, a little imp.

The chemistry failed in the first photo session, and the expressions seemed forced and tentative. The session which followed with the boy

could hardly have gone better. Greg was cute, and he knew it. But an immediate rapport with Kelly and a strong hint of mischief in his eyes produced several shots which appeared entirely unposed.

It was the most difficult of these which was chosen for the carving. It was the shot which evidenced the greatest joy and spontaneity, but it also posed the greatest danger, as the differences between such a laugh and a pained grimace are subtle and delicate, particularly on a child and in such a small scale. Equally onerous was the fact that it was a tilted three-quarter profile, for if the sculptor of a relief wishes to maintain the exact profile he must attack the face only from the angle of the camera until such time as he is absolutely certain that it will need no further recessing or redefining of those contours which were visible to the camera. (The difficulty comes when

Butternut, 21" wide x 23" high x 4-1/2" thick, 1990
Collection of Dennis and Joyce Kamstra
#280

the artist views the carved head from an angle and his eye tells him that it is entirely wrong. Working on the far side of the face will immediately make it appear more natural, but it will also destroy the pattern profile and eliminate the possibility of further recessing the face in order to make it as correct as possible.)

All in all things went as well as could be hoped, save for the fact of some discoloration in the wood which adversely affected both faces. The darkest ring was lightly masked with some oil paint. The initial finish of non-photoreactive tung oil was followed with coats of lightly stained photoreactive oil on the lighter areas and some selective ultraviolet degradation of the dark spots.

The full title of this piece is "'Tis in a Strange Bar Late, and the Lady Caressing His Thigh is not the Woman of His Dreams".

His exterior is not always the portrait of the inner man. A man is generally obliged to face confrontation and adversity with fearless bravado, but strange things happen in the game of sex when the male finds that the lady is the aggressor, and not necessarily to his liking. He may act disdainful and ferocious on the outside, but chances are that he is genuinely terrified within.

This piece was inspired by the woes of a fellow undergraduate at the U of Chicago back in the late '60s. It is not a self-portrait, though it is often confused as such since the model used was primarily the one in my mirror. Both parts of this carving are, of course, masks.

Butternut and Black Walnut
25" tall x 19" wide x 8" deep, 1989
#236

Another Beer at Rosie's

Ideas for a bar scene have been kicking around in my head for a full decade now, but each and every study was botched by my blundering ineptitude in using a flash with my camera. Then, in early '90, fellow carver John Burke, a character for whom there are no apt metaphors, talked me into being the artist in residence for a Western, Wildlife and Carving Workshop he was organizing for that summer. That, in conjunction with a familiarity with the number of fine neighborhood bars which dot the sidestreets of old Davenport, provided the impetus to try my flash once more.

Both of us were conducting seminars at the Congress. On Thursday evening John and his wife, Nancy, and I wandered off for a Pizza and some test shots at the Meatmarket — then meandered across the street to check out the scene at the Northwest Turners'. The latter facility was established as part of an old German Gymnastics and Athletic Club, which should come as no surprise, as bending the elbow has long been fabled to be the favorite Teutonic exercise.

As fate would have it, my previous sheer idiocy was now reduced to mere stupidity and ineptitude. The best shots were unusable for lack of exposure. But one of John, the barkeep, and a stranger seemed to have some promise. The print was first reversed right for left. The stranger was by and large OK, but John was looking in the wrong direction and appeared too young anyway — so I took off his head and put on another one more to my liking. The bartender was indistinct and required manufacturing. The bank of cigarettes behind him was uninspiring, to say the least, so it was replaced with a fictitious classical backbar featuring a painting by Jacopo Tintoretto, a 16th century Italian master.

The foreground was originally intended to be crossed

The original sketch used for Another Beer at Rosie's.

sheaves of grain as one might find on a number of beer labels, but it was later decided that 19th century illustrations of the vintner's trade made better models, and that the sheaves of grain would be secondary.

"Another Beer" saw two good days of work at the John Burke Workshop mentioned above, and another couple of days of token effort when returning home, before finding itself on the backburner until '91. The photo shows it in an "in-progress" state.

Butternut, 22" wide x 5" thick, 1991
#289

Afterword

A number of individuals who have received personal correspondence from the author have anticipated (feared) a book written in the style of his letters. In order to placate those readers (and to confuse others) we include the following conclusion, written in pure "Cogelese".

Post Lewd

It haz bin lepht too mee, Phillip B. Anderer, two iksplane too the reederz of this boock az two why it wur knot ritten inn the stile whitch iz custom merry four Fred when Cora S. Ponding with hiz piers. Mayke won thing cleer, that oppshin wuz wayed, end the awthur wint sew far az two right a knice I'll peece awn how, in hiz kollidge daze, he wuz sew congphewzed bigh thoze awe stenssibully owe posed two whar yelleen "giv Pizza Chants!", that he endid up a wouldcarver.

Wel, woodent ewe no, the editur, Missed Her Mishkaw, coudent evin sett it two tipe without Miss Spelleen "proktallijissed," which sirtinlee wuz the crucks of Phred's epissel awn hiz edjewkayshun. The right Een wuz awn the wahl, sew two speek, end evin migh sekwretarry, Ms. Anne Thrope, coud sea end khanquerred that it maid know cents two pub lishh sumtheen sew prophouwned if the editur wood leev it awl Miss Spelt! Kidz theez daze r bean taut that it iz the cow moonicashun uv eye deeahs, knot spelleen, whitch iz impotent, end hoo nose, meighbee sumdeigh the editurz' spellen will bee good enuf; butt four now, wir uv the ould skool, end iph we kant dew it write, we woughdnt dew it at awl!

since early,

Phillip B. Anderer

President, Phillip B. Anderer
Enterprises, Ltd.

(Note: Rural Virtue, Ltd., is a holy-owned subsidiary of Phillip B. Anderer Enterprises).

About the Artist

Frederic Cogelow (rhymes with Michelangelo) was born in Willmar, Minnesota on October 23, 1949, the 4th in a family of six children. Fred graduated from the University of Chicago in 1971 with a Bachelor's degree in Political Science. He then returned to Willmar and began a series of jobs working with young children and disturbed adolescents. A late 1975 hiatus from this work led inadvertently to his first attempt at professional woodworking. Economic realities brought him back to the job market in 1977 when he became a four-county CETA Youth Programs Coordinator. The desire to become his own boss led him to try carving again on a full-time basis in 1978.

Fred lives in the house in which his parents lived, along with his wife, Doris, and their dog, Toozer. Doris is employed by the Kandiyohi County Community Health Service as a nurse.

Fred's studio-workshop, located immediately behind his home, was a country chicken-coop which he dismantled in 1977 and reassembled in town as a lumber-drying shed. In 1982 it was remodeled into the present two-story building, with the lower floor housing power equipment and lumber. The second floor contains his carving studio, office, and a room for storing and controlling moisture content of his carving stock. With the trees growing around and through the upper story deck, a visitor climbing the outside stairway gets the feeling of entering a tree house.

Doris, Fred, and Toozer

Fred accepts commissions infrequently, preferring instead to pursue his own ideas and dreams. The difficult and demanding nature of the medium (wood), and of his designs, mark him as a perfectionist — and insures that he will have few, if any, successful imitators. All of his works are one-of-a-kind pieces, executed directly in the wood without first using models in clay or wax. With the exception of a very few early works, his pieces bear the trademark symbol shown at the top-right corner of the pages of this book. Those created since 1982 are sequentially numbered.

Fred's works are the result of his

own efforts entirely, from cutting the tree to applying the protective finish on the completed carving. For many years he found that the joys of procuring logs and bringing them to Harold Strand's sawmill far exceeded the pleasure of actually carving the by-product — and so he has accumulated a considerable quantity of hardwood lumber

Fred's workshop-studio.

which he stores in old barns around the Willmar area. Even now, with enough stock to last him several lifetimes, he has a difficult time passing up any decent butternut or walnut trees, particularly if they are otherwise headed for decay or a firewood pile.

In the process of his work Fred has developed a new design for carving gouges. This design incorporates an angled cutting edge which gives the gouge a shearing action as it cuts through the wood, resulting in greater efficiency and control. These gouges, named the Cogelow skew-gouges, are now being manufactured by the Henry Taylor Tool Company of Sheffield, England and sold to serious woodcarvers throughout the world.

It was just 18 years ago that Fred first started woodcarving, and he has accomplished a great deal in that time. Now, with this experience and expertise in hand, and at the relatively young age of 41, he is poised to take woodcarving to new and different heights. It will be exciting to see where he leads us.

Bob Mischka
Heart Prairie Press
1991

Major Awards

1990   **Congress** — People's Choice Award on "Gust —With Thoughts of Mabel"
       CNE — Show cancelled
       Silver Dollar City — Best of Show on "Gust — With thoughts of Mabel"
       Minnesota State Fair Fine Arts Exhibition — People's Choice
            Award on "Gust — With Thoughts of Mabel"

1989   **Congress** — People's Choice Award and Second Best of Show on
           "Lollie and Burt"
       CNE — Second Best of Show with "'Tis in a Strange Bar Late"
       Silver Dollar City — Best of Show on "Lollie and Burt"

1988   **Congress** — Second People's Choice Award and Second Best of
           Show with "Rural Requiem"
       CNE — Served as Judge — No Carvings entered
       Silver Dollar City — Best of Show on "Married Her in '33"

1987   **Congress** — Best of Show and People's Choice Award on "Married
           Her in '33", Third Best of Show with "Kilroy was Here Too"
       CNE — Best of Show on "Married Her in '33", Second Best of Show
          with "Easter Relief"
       Silver Dollar City — Best of Show on "Day's End"

1986   **Congress** — People's Choice Award on "Day's End"
       CNE — Second Best of Show on "Day's End"

1985   **Congress** — Best of Show on "Hunts the Crying Bear"
       CNE — Best of Show on "Old Man Kench"
          Runner-up to Best of Show on "Waiting to Swing"

1984   **CNE** — First Runner-up to Best of Show on "Hunts the Crying Bear"

1983   **CNE** — Best of Show on "The Hired Men"

Fred's domination of the relief carving category has been complete with the exception of the 1984 CNE. He received every "Best of Relief Group" award at the Congress from 1983 - 1987. Beginning in 1988 he was no longer eligible for that award but has entered the only relief carvings to make Best of Show since that time. All of his top awards at the CNE were with reliefs except in 1984. Each of his Silver Dollar City (1987–1990) Best of Show awards were with relief carvings except for 1990, where he won it with "Gust".

Major Awards (continued)

"Congress" is the Affilliated Woodcarvers Congress held in Davenport, Iowa, each June. This is the oldest, biggest and best woodcarving competition in the U.S.

"CNE" is the International Woodcarving Exposition held each August in Toronto. In recent years it has become the largest and best woodcarving competition held in North America. Held in conjunction with the Canadian National Exposition. (CNE).

"Silver Dollar City" is the Woodcarver's Showcase competition held at the Silver Dollar City Theme park in Branson, Mo., each September. This show began in 1987, and attracts entires from many of the top woodcarvers in the U.S. and Canada.

Photo Credits

The photo for "The Secret is Stealth" was provided by the carving's owner, Dr. Jon Bosland. The photos of Fred carving "Hunts Crying Bear" used as endpapers to the book, as well as the "Waitin' to Swing" photos, were taken by Ron Germanson. The "Decadent Bachelor Headboard" and the in-progress photo of "Rural Requiem" were taken by Fred Cogelow. The remaining photos were taken by Bob Mischka.

Index of Carvings

Sculptor in Wood